Rumor and Gossip

Rumor and Gossip

THE SOCIAL PSYCHOLOGY OF HEARSAY

Ralph L. Rosnow/Gary Alan Fine

ELSEVIER

New York/Oxford/Amsterdam

ELSEVIER SCIENTIFIC PUBLISHING COMPANY, INC.
52 Vanderbilt Avenue, New York, NY 10017

ELSEVIER SCIENTIFIC PUBLISHING COMPANY
335 Jan Van Galenstraat, P.O. Box 211
Amsterdam, The Netherlands

Portions of chapter 2 on the McCartney rumor were adapted from
an article by Rosnow and Fine [214]. Reprinted by permission ©
1974 *Human Behavior* Magazine.

Portions of chapters 2–4 were drawn from an article written for
the *Journal of Communication* [213]. Material copyrighted by the
Annenberg School of Communication of the University of Pennsylvania.

Lyrics of "I am the Walrus" and "Glass Onion" by John Lennon
and Paul McCartney © 1967 and © 1968 Northern Songs Ltd. All
rights for United States, Canada, Mexico, and Philippines controlled by Maclen Music, Inc. Reprinted by permission.

Material in Appendix originally appeared as an in-house memorandum for the Community Relations Service, Department of Justice. This edited and slightly abridged version is published by
permission of the author, A.A. Peltz, and the Justice Department.

Figures 4 and 5 from *The Psychology of Rumor* by Gordon W.
Allport and Leo Postman. Copyright 1947 by Holt, Rinehart and
Winston, Inc. Adapted and reprinted by permission of Leo Post-
man and the publisher.

Library of Congress Cataloging in Publishing Data

Rosnow, Ralph L
    Rumor and gossip: The Social Psychology of Hearsay

    Bibliography: p.
    Includes index.
    1. Rumor. 2. Gossip. I. Fine, Gary Alan,
joint author. II. Title.
HM263.R585   301.11   76-25446
ISBN 0-444-99031-3
    0-444-99035-6 pbk

MANUFACTURED IN THE UNITED STATES OF AMERICA

Designed by Loretta Li

Contents

Preface

Rumor and gossip have been of perennial interest in sociology and anthropology. Lately they have attracted considerable popular interest, stimulated by revelations of White House happenings during the Watergate episode, C.I.A. and F.B.I. disclosures of domestic wiretapping and other American clandestine activities at home and abroad. It is surprising, despite the pervasiveness of and wide interest in both phenomena in society, that rumor receives only passing attention in psychology and gossip none at all.

This work attempts to remedy the situation by exploring several levels of inquiry on both subjects, with the aim of developing an elementary integrative model to account for their social psychological bases. Thus the book may be read by students of collective behavior, communications, speech, general sociology, and social psychology in courses stressing an eclectic orientation. It will also be of interest to lay readers seeking an introductory statement on the nature and treatment of hearsay. To reach this diverse audience we have tried to interpolate the pertinent statistical data in a relatively unobtrusive style which will neither distract from the flow of the discussion nor dilute the exposition of research findings.

We are indebted to many people for help and encouragement in various stages of this project. We thank Uriel G. Foa, George Gerbner, Jeffrey H. Goldstein, and David Kipnis for valuable editorial suggestions on a preliminary draft, and Robert F. Bales for comments on a derivative manuscript. Donald Allport Bird discussed issues covered in the relationship of rumor to popular culture and folklore, helping us to conceptualize them within a social psychological frame of reference. Susan Anthony, Marianne Jaeger Biberian, Robert F. Gordon, and A. George Gitter collaborated with the first author in gathering experimental and correlational data and were helpful in locating primary source materials for the bibliography, as were Gordon W. Russell, Roberta McConochie, Patricia Castell, and Allan Kimmel. The first author also expresses his appreciation to Temple University for generous research support, especially for a summer fellowship awarded during the final stage of this project, and to Sandy Candeub for her invaluable assistance. Finally, we owe a very special debt of gratitude to Mimi Rosnow and Susan Fine for their conscientious support, editorial advice, and assistance throughout this endeavor.

RALPH L. ROSNOW
GARY ALAN FINE

hear·say (hēr'sā'), *n.* 1. unverified, unofficial information gained or acquired from another and not part of one's direct knowledge: *I pay no attention to hearsay.* 2. an item of idle or unverified information; gossip; rumor: *a malicious hearsay*

The Random House Dictionary
of the English Language

RUMOR. Common talk; current story passing from one person to another without any known authority for the truth of it; flying or popular report; general public report of certain things, without any certainty as to their truth.

"Rumor" has been held equivalent to, or synonymous with, "hearsay". . . .

Corpus Juris Secundum

gos'sip (gŏs'ĭp), *n.* [AS. *godsibb,* fr. *god* God + *sibb* related, a relation.] 1. *Archaic.* a A godparent. b A friend; crony. 2. An idle tattler; a newsmonger. 3. A gossip's tattle; groundless rumor; also, chatter. . . .

Webster's New Collegiate Dictionary

Rumor and Gossip

one : : "Anesthetic Prowler On Loose"

Everybody says it, and what everybody says must be true.

JAMES FENIMORE COOPER
Miles Wallingford

Talk is cheap, so the popular expression goes; yet hearsay can be a precious commodity in the marketplace of social exhange. Its value lies in its myriad functions. It can titillate the imagination, comfort or excite, manipulate or maintain the status quo. When skepticism is low and gullibility high, hearsay can provoke people to do and believe incredible things.

The curious case of the "phantom anesthetist of Mattoon" illustrates some of these remarkable properties. The episode, later documented by Professor Donald M. Johnson in the *Journal of Abnormal and Social Psychology* [124], began on a peaceful evening in September 1944 in Mattoon, Illinois (population 15,827). Around midnight a resident, Mrs. A, believing that a prowler had opened her bedroom window and sprayed her and her daughter with a paralyzing, mawkish gas, had her neighbor telephone the town police. They arrived al-

most immediately, but could detect no signs of an intruder.
Two hours later Mr. A arrived home and reported to the police
that he had just seen a man running from the vicinity of the
bedroom window. Again the police searched the grounds, but
found nothing. The following evening the local newspaper carried a front-page story under the column heading "Mrs. A and
Daughter First Victims." The headline on page one read
"Anesthetic Prowler on Loose."

The phrase "First Victims" became a self-fulfilling
prophecy. Throughout the following week, one report after
another of prowlers and phantom gassers came into police
headquarters. A massive effort was made to catch the elusive
prowler. Some of the townsfolk, armed with shotguns, sat on
their doorsteps and waited for him to strike again. Others believed they had caught a glimpse of him pumping away with
his spray gun. The number of reports grew and soon exhausted
the facilities of the local police department. The state police
were summoned in hopes that their radio-equipped squad cars
and scientific crime detection equipment could aid in the
search. In at least three cases, people reported that family dogs
had also been gassed—since none had barked at the intruder.
Before long the story appeared in out-of-town newspapers and
radio and press reports around the world. One paper wrote:

> Groggy as Londoners under protracted aerial blitzing, this town's
> bewildered citizens reeled today under the repeated attacks of a
> mad anesthetist who has sprayed a deadly nerve gas into 13 homes
> and has knocked out 27 victims. . . . Seventy others dashing to the
> area in response to the alarm, fell under the influence of the gas
> last night. . . . All skepticism vanished and Mattoon grimly con-
> ceded it must fight haphazardly against a demented phantom ad-
> versary who has been seen only fleetingly and so far has evaded
> traps laid by city and state police and posses of townsmen.

Worried American servicemen stationed as far away as New
Guinea and India wrote home to Mattoon, anxious to establish
that their families were safe.

The episode ended as mysteriously as it began. The number
of telephone calls to the Mattoon Police Department about
prowlers and phantom gassers slackened and finally stopped.
Without direct evidence to confirm the gasser's existence, the

major newspapers reversed their position on the story. Editorials now expressed skepticism that the prowler ever existed (although the townspeople maintained the truth of the tale). In time the bizarre details became rather ridiculous when studied dispassionately. Taken one by one, the "facts" seemed to evaporate in thin air.

First, the symptoms of the gasser's "victims" were remarkably like the classic psychiatric description of hysteria: nausea and vomiting, sudden and temporary paralysis of the limbs, palpitations, dryness of the mouth and throat. In fact, all those who were sent to the hospital for diagnosis were identified as suffering from hysteria. Second, there was no physical trace of his presence. Although the police acted quickly and diligently, they could not uncover direct evidence of any suspects or apparent motives. Third, the chemistry of the gas had a contradictory nature. It would have to be a very potent, stable anesthetic with unusually rapid action, yet at the same time sufficiently unstable so that it did not always have the same toxic effect. It had to be powerful enough to bring on paralysis and vomiting, but leave no observable traces. According to experts, no such concoction existed outside science fiction or the imagination. The most plausible interpretation is that the episode was a contagious emotional outburst based on hearsay, apprehension, and suggestibility. Any number of experiences could have served as triggering mechanisms: the trauma of World War II, the popularity of a crime novel or radio drama, a general malaise or fear of the future. Apparently, events combined with the personalities of the original "victims" to produce this striking hysterical epidemic.

Many similar episodes are recorded in the annals of psychiatry and sociology, incidents in which hearsay and autosuggestion combine to produce a contagion of hysteria. In the tri-state Pennsylvania-Ohio-West Virginia region in the 1960s, there was talk that gonorrhea detected in a public elementary school was likely to become an epidemic [161]. Although there was no evidence of this disease, the rumor grew to mammoth proportions and eventually forced officials to quarantine the school. In Detroit, Michigan, in the winter of 1967–68, a grisly horror tale gripped the population in a city already filled with fear, hatred, and trepidation from racial riots the summer before [211]. It was rumored that a young boy, shopping with his mother in a downtown department store, went into a lavatory where he was attacked and castrated. In the story the race of the victim and perpetrators of the crime were always in opposition, while the teller of the story was usually of the same race as the victim. The castration myth is an old tale which appears throughout history in many variants, but this in no way eased the tensions of those who heard it for the first time. This rumor, too, was completely unfounded.

In this work we intend to show some of the ways people respond to hearsay, and to examine its psychological and sociological properties. In particular we shall explore the dimensions of the familiar phenomena of rumor and gossip which, in various definitions—legal and common—are held synonymous with hearsay. We shall argue, however, that in form (if not also in function) rumor and gossip are not always equivalent concepts. Rumor is information, neither substantiated nor refuted; gossip is small talk with or without a known basis in fact. The multiple functions that both serve are practically identical, but the motivational hierarchies appear to be different: rumors seem most often fueled by a desire for meaning, a quest for clarification and closure; gossip seems motivated primarily by ego and status needs. There are also differences in conceptualization of the same phenomenon, colored by different epistemological assumptions. The favored psychological model of rumormongering is linear: it involves serial chains made up of connecting links symbolizing proximate individual needs. In contrast, the preferred sociological model of rumormongering is latticelike: the interstitial points again represent individual responses, but the main emphasis is on collective instrumental actions.

We seek to identify, order, and categorize thematic elements in rumor and gossip as a way to construct a unified interpretation. Underlying elements in the concepts, methods, propositions, and hypotheses can be used to identify themata inductively, and it is possible to submit some of these to a test which examines and incorporates the flow of experimental data available [cf. 112, 113, 170]. The basic theme uniting the various levels of interpretation is that of social exchange. Following recent work by Homans, the Foas, Thibaut and Kelley, and Paine, we use the concept of exchange as a metaphor for the way human interaction proceeds, fully realizing that man is not a totally rational animal, and without suggesting that a process akin to Jeremy Bentham's hedonic calculus is operating. However, human behavior functions *as if* it operates on the basis of social exchange, and in many instances people do maneuver in this fashion. Giving and receiving, in order to be stable and predictable, follows a regular pattern of outcomes mediated by needs, emotions, instincts, and expectations.

In chapter 2, rumor is etymologically and analytically dissected. By way of an introduction to stages in the life cycle, the Paul McCartney rumor is presented in some detail. This is a particularly interesting example of hearsay because of its androgynous characteristics; it qualifies as both rumor and gossip.

In chapter 3 we describe what is known about stages and patterns in the evolution and disintegration of a rumor. Some rumors occur spontaneously, others are carefully constructed by propagandists and other manipulators. Once started, a rumor is transmitted in much the same way as information carried by neural impulses in the human nervous system. It passes from person to person at a speed which is dependent on the social chemistry. The way the rumor ends depends on the nature of the tale; some rumors never die, but become part of the folklore and established belief structure—for example, the spate of rumors surrounding John F. Kennedy's assassination. However, most rumors are born, thrive for a time, and then disappear because they were disproved, or became irrelevant, or people grew weary of them.

To understand the nature of rumor requires a close analysis of the different viewpoints of social scientists as discussed in chapter 4. There is not always simple agreement on the primary function or purpose of rumor, and it is possible that each of the interpretations surveyed in this chapter represents a part of the truth. One is reminded of the Yiddish anecdote about the dayyan, or rabbinical judge, who was asked by a couple to mediate a lingering controversy in which they were embroiled. The woman told her story, and the dayyan commented, "You are right." Then the man told his side, and the dayyan responded, "You are right." A young student, overhearing the conversations, pointed out to the dayyan, "Surely they both cannot be a hundred percent right." To which the dayyan replied: "You are right, too." The disagreement on the function of rumor can be better adjudicated by emphasizing the similarities in viewpoints than by arguing that any single interpretation is valid or invalid for all cases. In dividing the different explanations according to the basic units of analysis, social exchange clearly emerges as a unifying theme.

In chapter 5 there is a discussion of the few experimental studies conducted on the function of rumor. With this evidence we begin to flesh out the integrative model. Other pertinent studies lead us further along the path of logical inference toward a more general statement on the transactional nature of rumormongering. We discover that there are striking similarities between the "rules" of hearsay and the principles of economic exchange.

Having examined the nature of rumor in some detail, we turn in chapter 6 to the examination of the nature of gossip. The life cycle of gossip is not as easily divisible as rumor into distinct stages, and the hierarchy of triggering conditions is probably different than that involving rumor. Like rumor, gossip has been studied from different perspectives, and not every observer agrees on its basic functions. However, the mortar of social exchange binds these interpretations as well.

How the mass media use both rumor and gossip is the subject of chapter 7. The press, television, radio, national and regional magazines play a part in the transmission, and sometimes in the origin, of these forms. They are indicators, but also pacesetters, of what is novel or current. They are also gatekeepers: they control the flow of news reports, and public access in drastically skewed in favor of the media. This raises the question of social responsibility: the media have a singular responsibility to report the news fairly and accurately; freedom of the press is not a license to invent news or to embellish the truth with tenuous hearsay.

In chapter 8 we consider the control of rumor and gossip. With a better understanding of the social psychology of hearsay, we can expect to discover more effective means of dealing with malicious forms. However, some situations are by nature persistently ripe for rumormongering, and no manner of corrective action will remove that vulnerability. One may not be able to attack etiological factors, but one can at least treat symptoms. Rumor control centers, inspired by World War II rumor clinics, have been the principal means to this end. The mechanics of rumor control are discussed, and the book concludes (see Appendix) with recommended standards for the operation of rumor control centers.

two :: Anatomy of a Rumor

> Rumor! What evil can surpass her
> speed? In movement she grows
> mighty, and achieves strength and
> dominion as she swifter flies.
>
> VERGIL
> *Aeneid*

Literary interest in the nature of rumor is deeply rooted, as these lines from the *Aeneid* testify; scientific interest in rumor is essentially a product of the 20th century. Since the early 1900s, rumor has been studied, analyzed, and reported on by scholars representing diverse areas of inquiry. Psychologists study the transmission process and the nature of recall; sociologists analyze rumor from the viewpoint of societal structure and the communication process; anthropologists and folklorists are intrigued for what is revealed about social control and rhetorical style; psychoanalysts see in rumor universal metaphors; historians attempt to unravel the effects that rumors have had in wars and economic crises; lawyers study rumor to understand the nature and limits of testimony; physicians work to understand its hysterical contagion; and the police and military attempt to prevent its violence and sabotage.

This disparity of viewpoints necessarily leads to diverse opinions on the worth and affective value of rumor. Some argue that it is a vital curative for society; others maintain that it is harmful, vile, and distasteful. To begin, we must ask what rumor is, and why it lends itself to different interpretations.

THE NATURE OF RUMOR

In Roman mythology, *Fama* was the personification of rumor—the Hellenic equivalent being *Ossa,* the messenger of Zeus. Thus Vergil noted: *fama volat* (rumor flies). Rumor has sometimes been called "Dame Rumor" (possibly a corruption of "damn rumor") as in the following first-hand account of a tragic experience which became indelibly fixed in the mind of U.S. Marine Corps General Smedley D. Butler [35, p. 24]:

The railroad has been mined. Bridges have been blown up. Hordes of fanatical Chinese are ambushed to massacre the Marines.... These and similar reports reached the small detachment of United States Marines in June, 1900, as we were about to start from Tangku, China, to the relief of Tientsin during the Boxer Rebellion. Natives and foreigners, hearing that we were determined to make the hazardous journey, rushed about our camp spreading stories they had heard of the fate that awaited us if we ever started for Tientsin.... Most Marines are hard-boiled and adventurous, but there were among us many young men with little, if any, war experience. Some of us were hardly more than boys and we really were frightened. One young Marine—he wasn't more than eighteen—raced from one native to another, seeking all the details of the reports they said had come from the Boxers. He wanted to know what might be expected if we were ambushed and he was captured. The natives gave details and bloodcurdling accounts of all the tortures to which captured enemies were subjected. This boy was soon on the verge of a breakdown.... We had a great leader there in Major (later General) Waller, and he gave the word to go—mined railroads and hordes of Chinese in ambush or not. We had seized a little native train, and Marines were running it. No sooner did the puffing locomotive get under way than a shot rang out. The excited young Marine, after hysterically shouting something about ambushes, shot himself through the heart. He died instantly.... And thus I learned about Dame Rumor and her evil, lying, trouble-making ways. For the reports were nothing but rumors. Whether they started maliciously or not, they spread with the rapidity with which only rumors are capable of traveling.

Not all who study rumor would agree with General Butler's characterization of it. However, most researchers concur on several attributes. Rumors are not facts, but hearsay: some rumors eventually prove to be accurate, but while they are in the stage described as "rumor" they are not yet verified. Rumors also are obviously a form of communication. Traditionally they were defined as products of face-to-face encounters. However, while many, perhaps most, of the rumors studied by social scientists fall in the category of word-of-mouth communication, limiting the concept to this channel would be an oversimplification disregarding the wide variety of potential media sources of rumor (and gossip). The press, because of its vast and heterogeneous audience, reaches many subgroups, socially and geographically. When newspapers report on a flying saucer sighting in one area of the country, during the next several weeks reports of flying saucers are legion.

A classic illustration is the rumor in 1938 of an invasion of Earth by men from the planet Mars [37]. The rumor originated in a dramatization over CBS Radio by Orson Welles of H. G. Wells' famous novel *The War of the Worlds*. The broadcast came within a month of the Munich crisis, and for weeks the American people had been listening closely to their radios for on-the-spot news coverage. This, combined with the sheer technical realism of the broadcast, created an atmosphere of apprehension and contagious suggestibility which swept across the United States.

Another, more recent, example is the incident in this country in 1972 in which the news media repeated a false report issued by columnist Jack Anderson (for which he later made a full apology and retraction). It was rumored by Anderson that Senator Thomas Eagleton, the Vice-Presidential nominee of the Democratic Party, had been arrested for drunken and reckless driving in the 1960s. The rumor surfaced around the same time that another intriguing report had just been confirmed, stating that Eagleton also had been treated by electro-shock therapy for a nervous disorder. This combination of news stories had the dramatic effect of forcing the Senator to resign from the Democratic national ticket. Norman Mailer has given the name "factoid" to these tales which are unfounded, but appear in the press and are repeated afterwards as facts [159].

A leading authority on the subject of rumor, Professor Tamotsu Shibutani, stresses that it is a vehicle for group problem solving [227]. Other investigators stipulate that rumor is partially defined by the primary channel in which it is transmitted—word of mouth—or imply that in order to constitute hearsay it must be spread in an unregimented fashion [21, 26]. Whether any of these views is sufficiently broad to encompass the definition of a factoid, as in the examples above, is problematical. Here we prefer a broader set of parameters in defining a rumor. First of all, it is a process of information dispersion as well as the product of that process. Secondly, it is a process that may be more easily started (and its product more easily disseminated) than stopped. Thirdly, it is a communication constructed around unauthenticated information. There is one additional distinguishing feature which is not usually mentioned: rumor is nonnormative evidence. Someone who repeats a rumor is transmitting suspect evidence. To be sure, a rumor may be entirely appropriate within the given circumstances, but the genre removed from its context is nonnormative. Hence, rumor is deviant on an ideal level even while being useful and conforming in practice.

Several of these characteristics will be reminiscent of other communication forms such as legend and gossip. In contrast to a legend, a rumor usually dwells on topical content, although some legends may reappear occasionally embodied in the form of a rumor. Gossip, as noted earlier, has an even clearer relation to rumor, and the terms are often used interchangeably. We shall argue that there is sufficient difference in meaning and, particularly in research, that an analytical distinction can be made. It was stated that the basis of gossip may or may not be a known fact, but the basis of rumor is always unsubstantiated. Also, gossip typically deals with the personal affairs of individuals, but rumors can also deal with events and issues of great importance or magnitude. While in our discussion of rumor we shall have occasion to speak of gossip, it is considered more fully in chapter 6.

Pejorative Connotation of Rumor

Rumor usually has a pejorative connotation implying mischief or scandal. General Butler claimed [35, p. 156]: "I'd rather fight an entire army than battle an idle rumor." While not all would concur with his priorities, many would certainly agree with his expansive statement (despite its perhaps "sexist" overtones) that, "She [Dame Rumor] can start wars, break friendships; she can cause annoyance and irritation; she is a tool often of the unscrupulous and the evil." Niehoff has defined a rumormonger as one who purveys "negative gossip," [180] and the *Random House Dictionary* refers to rumor as "a malicious hearsay." The Yiddish word for rumormonger, *yenta,* is defined as a female gossip or scandal-spreader [216]. In the Old Testament the prophet Ezekiel warns: "Mischief shall come upon mischief, and rumor shall be upon rumor; then shall they seek a vision of the prophet; but the law shall perish from the priest, and counsel from the ancients." The *Report of the National Advisory Commission on Civil Disorders* concluded [136, p. 326]: "Rumors significantly aggravated tensions and disorder in more than 65 percent of the disorders studied by the Commission."

This sounds awfully distressing. Yet Shibutani can argue that rumor is a form of group problem solving that is not only *not* pathological but an essential part of the social process; rumors allow human beings to cope with the uncertainties of life. Others stress that rumormongering is not merely the product of idle curiosity but an aid to individuals or groups to gain functional ends [77]. Some argue that rumormongering reflects the normal desire to find meaning in events even though the attempt might prove dysfunctional [10, 144]. Keith Davis discovered in his study of organizational grapevines an expression of the healthy, natural human motivation to communicate [57, pp. 261, 263]: "In fact, if employees are so uninterested in their work that they do not engage in shoptalk about it, they are probably maladjusted. If employees are so uninterested in their associates that they do not exchange talk about who will likely get the next promotion or who recently had a baby, they probably are abnormal."

This disparity of views is traceable largely to the observer's frame of reference. When one studies rumor in a panic situation, such as in natural disasters, a feeling that rumormongering is harmful is nearly inescapable (even though one is sympathetic with the population's striving for security and certainty). In wars and in riots, where social control is deemed essential, informal social communication that militates against control will likely be frowned upon. Steps will be taken, indeed laws may be passed, to suppress rumormongering. However, even in peacetime there are instances of anti-rumor legislation: it is against the law in this country to make, circulate, or transmit any "rumor, written, printed, or by word of mouth, which is untrue in fact and is directly or by inference derogatory to the financial condition or affects the solvency or financial standing of the Federal Savings and Loan Insurance Corporation" (U.S. Code Annotated, 1966, Ch. 47, 18–1009). That it is now illegal to spread rumors on the floor of the stock exchange, even when no overt fraud is intended (Rule 435 of the New York Stock Exchange and Rule 3c of the American Stock Exchange), is also indicative of the power of rumors when left unchecked. This was certainly true in the 1920s when speculators routinely used journalists to spread stories and plant ideas. Rumors were rampant in the securities markets, and there were reports of bribes being given to newspapermen to publicize stocks during this wildly speculative and calamitous period [235].

In recent years many social scientists, sociologists in particular, have sought to refrain from casting value judgments on human behavior on the grounds that any regularly occurring behavior must have some useful purpose. The task of the social scientist is to discover functions, not to disparage or to criticize. Rumor sometimes produces outcomes which are unfortunate, but the concept is neutral; it takes on whatever values are inherent in the situation.

Consider the Paul McCartney rumor [214], a story quite different from the phantom anesthetist of Mattoon. This rumor, too, possesses all the classic characteristics: the incident began casually, quickly circulated, and remained stubbornly persistent even in the face of contradictory evidence. However, any negative or malicious effects were minimal; the rumormongering appears to have served definite, positive social functions.

THE PAUL MCCARTNEY RUMOR

Like many rumors and legends, when and where the story first developed is uncertain. We are told that it was started in 1967 by a guru-type at Eastern Michigan University in Ypsilanti, picked up by the local counterculture for a time, and then dropped to lay dormant for two years. Its origin is also in part traceable to a newspaper article, which may qualify the rumor as a factoid.

Perhaps it surfaced publicly for the first time on the afternoon of 12 October 1969 when disc jockey Russ Gibb of Detroit radio station WKNR-FM received a telephone call on the air from a young man identified as Tom who described some remarkable coincidences. If the Beatles' song "Revolution Number 9" is played backwards and one listens carefully to the voice saying, "Number 9, Number 9, Number 9" the words magically become: "Turn me on, dead man! . . ." At the end of the song "Strawberry Fields" in their *Magical Mystery Tour* album, when the background noises are filtered out, there is someone saying: "I buried Paul!"

Two days after Gibb's radio broadcast, the University of Michigan newspaper, *The Michigan Daily,* appeared with the legend in the masthead: "McCartney Is Dead." The full-page headline on page two read "McCartney Dead; New Evidence Brought to Light," and was followed by an article of 58 column inches by Fred LaBour who had been assigned to review the Beatles' record album, *Abbey Road.* LaBour's article was accompanied by a gruesome picture of a bloody, decapitated head looking like Paul McCartney, and the article stated: "Paul McCartney was killed in an automobile accident in early November 1966, after leaving EMI recording studios tired, sad, and dejected." The story went on to detail how McCartney had been replaced by a double. LaBour, like the mysterious youngster Tom, also discovered some curious references, for instance:

(a) The album cover of *Sgt. Pepper* shows the lower part of a grave with yellow flowers shaped to resemble Paul McCartney's bass guitar, or possibly the letter "P". Inside the album cover McCartney wears an arm-patch reading OPD, for Officially Pronounced Dead. The medal on his chest commemorates heroic death. On the back cover everyone is facing forward, except for Paul McCartney.

(b) The album cover of *Abbey Road* (see FIG. 1) shows John Lennon dressed in white to resemble a minister, Ringo Starr dressed as an undertaker, George Harrison as a gravedigger, and McCartney barefoot to suggest the way

FIGURE 1. Album photograph from the cover of the Beatles' *Abbey Road*, showing (left to right) George Harrison, Paul McCartney, Ringo Starr, and John Lennon. The Beatles, rumored to be leaving a cemetery, were said to be dressed in the clothes of a gravedigger, a corpse, an undertaker, and a minister. The Volkswagen "Beetle" parked along the roadside carries a license plate reading "28 IF"—rumored to be a clue to Paul McCartney's age *if* he had survived. *(Reproduced by permission of EMI Records Limited)*

some corpses are buried in England. The Beatles are leaving a cemetery, according to reports. A Volkswagen Beetle parked along the road carries the license plate 28 IF—how old McCartney would have been *if* he had lived.

Following these incidents—the strange telephone call to Gibb and the provocative newspaper story by LaBour—the rumor of Paul McCartney's death caught fire. It whipped across the country, fueled by innuendoes and ambiguities. In a widely cited book on the psychology of rumor [10], Gordon W. Allport and Leo Postman argue that the foundation of rumors is laid when events are important and news is lacking or ambiguous. For the millions of American youth caught up in the Paul McCartney rumor these elements certainly seemed to characterize the psychological circumstances surrounding the story.

Soon, countless additional oddities began to be reported as the story rapidly disseminated. New meanings were attributed to things that seemed perfectly innocent and insignificant before the rumor appeared. The collection of symbols now included the *Magical Mystery Tour* picture with Ringo, John and George sporting red carnations and Paul wearing a black one. It was rumored that if one of the Beatles' albums was placed in water, the apple insignia would turn blood red. A series of inferences based upon the figure of the walrus supposedly symbolized death [238]. It is Paul (or his double) who in *I Am the Walrus* sings: "I am he as you are he as you are me and we are all together. I *am* the walrus." In the later "double white" album, *The Beatles,* John Lennon sings in "Glass Onion": "Well, here's another *clue* for all/The walrus *was* Paul." Indeed, "Glass Onion" is said to be filled with numerous clues announcing Paul's demise.

Actually, the newspaper photograph of the look-alike decapitated head was a hoax. So was the report of the car crash. There is no reasonable evidence for believing that Paul McCartney died. That the Beatles had planted "clues" is more believable, despite denials by McCartney at the time (*Life Magazine,* November 7, 1969) and John Lennon later (*Rolling Stone,* January 7, 1971). Plausible explanations, often rumors themselves, exist for many of these oddities. "I buried Paul"—this could have been someone saying that the music, being loud or distracting, had buried Paul's sound; the voice resembles that of John Lennon. On *Abbey Road* the Beatles are wearing their "ordinary" clothes. OPD is also said to be a badge picked up from the Ontario Police Department while the Beatles were on a Canadian tour. The parked Volkswagen, the mysterious pictures, the lyrics that only make sense when played backwards—these could all have been coincidence. But, whatever the explanations, it became the foundation for a fantasy that swept across American adolescent society, developing from a basic core, adding numerous variants, deviations, and new explanations as each person and group attempted to make sense of the "evidence" at hand.

Cultural Implications

Examining any rumor in retrospect can reveal much about the culture where it flourished and about the nature of truth in that culture. To the extent that the Paul McCartney rumor is found believable, it may imply that the world and in particular the mass media are deceptive. That generation of American youth had been brought up in the shadow of the John F. Kennedy assassination and the considerable doubt focused on the Warren Commission report. The credibility gap of Lyndon B. Johnson's presidency, the widely circulated rumors after the assassinations of Martin Luther King, Jr. and Robert F. Kennedy, as well as attacks on the leading media sources by the Yippies and Vice-President Spiro Agnew, no doubt help to foster an attitude in which a massive media conspiracy is plausible. A person of world renown can be replaced by another for three years without any of his audience being the wiser. As sociologist Erving Goffman has noted, a public identity is something that can be managed by a series of strategies [94, 95].

One need not assume that most of the rumor's audience believed that Paul McCartney was dead; but they did consider the question, thus lending credence to the rumor. One can also see the influence of the "underground" and student media. It was primarily FM-rock stations, college newspapers, and word of mouth which kept the rumor alive and growing through the discovery of new evidence. This provided a rumor network quite different from that in "adult" society; the establishment media spread a version of the tale colored with worldly cynicism. A boomerang effect occurred when *Life* published Paul McCartney's first-hand denial. The cover showed a picture of him which, coincidentally, had an automobile advertisement on the reverse side. Holding the cover up to the light revealed a car superimposed across McCartney's chest so that the top of his head was blocked out. This provided another basis for innuendo.

The mistrust of the establishment media leads to the question of how truth can be gauged by the rumor's audience. The "standard" measure of truth—"If I read it in the newspaper, it must be true"—is not always reliable or valid. Routine assumptions about practical epistemology also are being questioned. This attitude makes clear that truth is only accepted when it is consistent with one's frame of reference. Information is processed in light of the assumptions one holds about the nature of the world, for knowledge is culturally determined. What is truth to one person may be part of a massive conspiracy to another.

Most people who heard the McCartney rumor probably did not believe that he had actually been killed, although many may have considered the possibility. What seems likely is that most young people felt it was an enormous "cosmic hoax" perpetuated by the Beatles. Perhaps the Beatles were testing their public to determine perceptiveness; or possibly the Beatles were attempting to allow their fans to learn the "truth" without directly admitting culpability. All of these hypotheses were prevalent during the course of the rumor.

Paul McCartney's "death" and the gossip surrounding it take on the form of a well-constructed murder mystery, in which both clues and puzzles are numerous. The evidence was staged so that a stream of new facts would be forthcoming. Historical truth is not something always established by direct means; rather it is gathered through its symbolic representations. These symbols have more true meaning than do vocal or visual representations. Indeed latter elements add to the tale: there was a University of Miami professor who announced that he had determined through scientific voice detector tests that there had been *three* Paul McCartneys. Symbols and the cognitive system into which they belong may be more crucial than the legal evidence of autopsies and probate. It becomes problematical whether one can trust one's eyes and ears, and of course one's surrogate eyes and ears—the mass media.

A particularly intriguing element is that of the look-alike. Stories of doubles for world leaders have been commonplace, from Napoleon to Hitler. Several years ago there was a double of Secretary of State Henry Kissinger discovered in Chicago; a circumstance which led the Nixon Administration to announce that no double would be used in diplomacy. After John Kennedy's assassination, talk of a Kennedy double and an Oswald double was common [194]. Hence, the idea of a duplicate Paul McCartney is not preposterous in terms of Western popular beliefs. Yet it attests to a "grand conspiracy"—to arrange for an identity change with the public remaining ignorant of the plot. Identity becomes a James Bond role to be switched when appropriate, and the truth of an identity becomes relative and capable of being questioned despite ego protestations.

Functions

As we have discussed the nature of the communications system in which the Paul McCartney rumor flourished and spread and the nature of truth implicit for its believers, we should discuss the nature and function of the rumor itself. We will return to this topic in Chapter 5 to outline more fully the view that rumor is essentially a resource in social exchange. An important attribute of the McCartney rumor, viewed in this light, is its amusement and entertainment value. In return for some other psychological resource, an entertaining rumor was passed.

This rumor seems equivalent to many other rumors we shall discuss as it was an attempt to resolve an unclear or ambiguous situation. Affectively, it is unlike many classic rumors. It supposedly reported bad news, yet very little grief or fear was felt; no orientation towards action was associated with the report. It had the makings of a budding legend or literary invention, rather than the news item it supposedly was [238]. However, for a rumor to sustain interest there must be a suspension of disbelief on the part of the participants. Thus perhaps the clearest function of the rumor is its entertainment value. It is great fun hunting for clues and talking about the mystery with friends. The Paul McCartney rumor may have flourished for the same reasons that mystery stories are popular, suspense without fear and emotional stimulation. It titillated the imagination.

Finally, some brief mention should be made of the death of this rumor. It is unclear exactly when a rumor can be officially pronounced dead—even today we will occasionally hear one of its forms, or at least the recall of McCartney's "death." Some factors are apparent of course. Rumors grow on new information and interpretations; even denials can serve this purpose (witness McCartney's futile denial in *Life*). After a period of time no new evidence was forthcoming: the Beatles stopped denying the story, and there were only so many album covers on which to hunt for clues.

We have argued that the clearest function of this rumor is its entertainment value. In a later chapter we discuss survey data collected at the time suggesting that another function is to bestow status upon the teller. Clearly there became a point of diminishing returns for both of these functions when nothing new could be added to the tale and any teller gained minimally or even lost status by continuing to be obsessed by the mystery. Also there was a point at which young people realized that the mystery would never be unraveled. It became an unsolvable puzzle, uninteresting and tedious. The level of ambiguity stabilized and the importance of the rumor decreased with the passage of time.

While very different in emotional impact from the story of the phantom anesthetist of Mattoon, the McCartney rumor nevertheless is similar in many respects to this and other reports that have been studied. Like all things that exist in time and space, a rumor has a life history. This life seems to be similar for all rumors. Several studies have focused on one rumor or related sets of rumors and followed the story through its development and death. Let us turn now to a consideration of the stages in the life span of a rumor.

three : : Life and Death of a Rumor

Rumor is a pipe
Blown by surmises, jealousies, conjectures,
And of so easy and so plain a stop
That the blunt monster with uncounted heads,
The still-discordant wavering multitude,
Can play upon it.

WILLIAM SHAKESPEARE
King Henry IV

Edgar Morin, the French sociologist, studied a rumor about the alleged disappearance in 1969 of young women in Orléans, a middle-class French city [176]. Young girls, according to this malicious tale, had been drugged and imprisoned by Jewish boutique proprietors and then shipped to foreign centers of prostitution. It was further rumored that Jews had bribed police and government officials to remain silent.

In fact, there was not a grain of truth' to the tale; no women were ever reported missing in Orléans. One explanation for the story is that it may have originated in a fictitious kidnapping plot vividly reported in the popular French tabloid magazine *Noir et Blanc*. The cover of this particular issue had shown an anonymous, threatening male holding a terrified young woman around the throat. A sequence of other posed pictures inside the magazine showed her being forcibly drugged, lying unconscious in a wicker trunk on board ship, and being coerced into prostitution at gunpoint. In Orléans the abduction rumor appears to have taken root in jealousies and prejudices directed at Jewish shopkeepers who prospered by catering to the tastes of the youth trade. Given the sick nature of the rumor, it is not surprising that Morin employed a disease metaphor for its life history: incubation, propagation, metastasis, opposition, resorption, residua, and germs.

The Wallenpaupack rumor is another tale with a documented life history [54]. When hurricane Diane splashed her way across Port Jervis, New York in 1955 a false alarm, triggered by an Associated Press report (unpublished, no less) about the Wallenpaupack dam breaking, quickly circulated throughout the city. The rumor alleged that a typhoid epidemic was imminent, and resulted in the hurried departure of a quarter of the population.

In the Seattle windshield pitting epidemic of 1954, residents of Seattle, Washington panicked at what they perceived to be windshield pittings supposedly caused by radioactive fallout from the Eniwetok H-bomb tests [166]. On further investigation the "pits" turned out to be harmless, little black particles that formed through the improper combustion of bituminous coal. Here, too, there is a carefully documented life history of the incident.

Reports of hysterical contagion often follow regular patterns, although in these cases the disease analogy is sometimes more than a metaphor, with everything except a biological base arguing for a medical diagnosis other than hysteria. From these case studies on the evolution and devolution of rumor, three general stages emerge: birth, adventures, and death.

STAGE 1—BIRTH

Because of the dominant role of motivation in the origin of rumor, form and function can be quite varied. Rumor may refer to a group effort to define what is occurring, or rumor may be a packaged story, deliberately planted. In the rumor in Orléans, speculations and sentiments swelled into a spiteful and nearly overpowering wave of hostility, feeding on jealousies and

anti-Semitic prejudices. In the Wallenpaupack rumor, suggestibility and false reporting precipitated a panic due to the prevailing sense of danger wrought by the storm. In the Seattle
windshield pitting epidemic, large numbers of people focused
on their car windshields rather than the field of vision beyond
them. In the McCartney rumor, which amused and enter-
tained, a whole generation of young people played detective,
attempting to piece together the parts of an intriguing puzzle.
Shakespeare captured this diverse and ephemeral nature of
rumor in his metaphor of a pipe blown by surmises, jealousies,
conjectures.

Several researchers have sought to develop a standard functional classification in order to pinpoint the predominant motivations which give birth to rumors [120, 188, 196, 227]. The
best known attempt was made by Robert H. Knapp during
World War II in conjunction with the Massachusetts Committee on Public Safety where Gordon Allport served as an ad-
visor [139]. Knapp, in 1942, secured a collection of rumors
through the auspices of the Boston Rumor Clinic and two mass
circulation magazines *Reader's Digest* and *American Mercury*.
The rumors were then analyzed and carefully sorted into three
broad categories termed pipe dreams, bogies, and wedge-
drivers. The pipe dream, or wish, rumor expresses a person's
hopes—for example, the rumor that Japan did not have enough
oil to last six months, or the frequent rumors of the war's end
and Hitler's death. The bogie rumor mirrors fear and
anxiety—"The entire Pacific Fleet was destroyed at Pearl Harbor." The wedge-driving, or aggression, rumor divides
groups—for example, the rumor that American Catholics were
trying to evade the draft. Of 1,089 rumors examined by Knapp,
the majority were wedge-drivers (66 percent)—only 2 percent
of the total were pipe dream rumors and 25 percent were
bogies (the remaining 7 percent were unclassified). Most
common among wedge-driving rumors were those directed
against the Administration and the Armed Forces, but 9 percent of all rumors were anti-Semitic and 3 percent anti-Negro.
We cannot know for certain if these percentages actually represented the population at large, but the figures strongly suggest that large numbers of aggressive and hateful rumors were
in circulation. Because such rumors had the capacity to lower

public morale, and also because of the danger of leaking secret information, there were repeated attempts to warn citizens of the problem in telling tales during wartime (see FIG. 2).

More recently, Knapp's typology was applied to another set of wartime rumors. Sociologist N. K. U. Nkpa, of the University of Nigeria, collected tales told by university students and by Biafran villagers and former urbanites who had taken shelter in rural areas during the Nigerian Civil War of 1967–1970 [181]. In contrast to Knapp's finding that pipe dream rumors are the rarest kind, Nkpa found that almost two-thirds of the tales he collected are of this variety. Wedge-driving rumors make up only 18 percent of the total, and bogie rumors 12 percent. These results, too, suggest the likelihood that wartime rumormongering is mediated by strong anxieties.

Both studies tell us something of the important role of motivational elements in the promulgation of rumors. However, when we search for a unitary or identifiable source of rumor, in hope of isolating the exact underlying motivation in the first place, we are not always successful. Indeed the common conception of the origin of rumor maintains it is impossible to establish the creator (as it is for most items of folklore). Certainly in the case of wedge-driving rumors during World War II or in the Nigerian Civil War it would probably have been counterproductive to the subversive aims of their creators to reveal who the true sources were. Where the listener is the passive recipient of information he or she "happens" to overhear, defenses are often low and vulnerability high [215, p. 353]. The rumormonger in psychological warfare will attempt to keep his true identity a secret in order that he may continue this impression management. In this strategy game, the enemy agent poses as a loyal citizen, and the host government's job is to uncover the rumor and the active and knowing participants before they can do damage to the national morale [162, 192, 218].

Much is known about the etiology of wartime rumors. The literature on this subject ranges from scholarly interest to shocked concern. War is the quintessential situation of apprehension and ambiguity, and there are countless illustrations of the contagious influence of pipe dreams, bogies, and wedge-drivers spreading with wild abandon. Because indi-

FIGURE 2. Second World War posters warning of the danger in telling tales during wartime. The poster on the left was drawn by the American artist John Atherton, that on the right by the Britisher Bruce Bairnsfather. *(Photographs courtesy of Imperial War Museum, London)*

viduals are forced to close ranks in confronting a common danger, collective sentiments are aroused [66]. In "the great Ipswich fright" of 1775, residents of Ipswich, Massachusetts panicked upon hearing a false bogie rumor that the Red Coats were coming; some citizens got as far away as Portsmouth, New Hampshire before sheepishly returning home. Early in 1941, Prince Paul of Yugoslavia, frightened by the ever-encroaching Nazi military machine and increasingly desperate to stave off an invasion, signed an accord with Hitler. British intelligence agents in Yugoslavia, passed exaggerated pipe dream rumors of British military strength in neighboring Greece and were able to foment a coup which resulted in the overthrow of the old Serbian regime and the gain of precious time.

Because of the emotional factors in war, the critical ability of much of the population is suspended or rather low. "O for a lodge in some vast wilderness," wrote English poet William Cowper during the Napoleonic period of the late eighteenth century:

Some boundless contiguity of shade,
Where rumors of oppression and deceit,
Of unsuccessful or successful war
Might never reach me more.

In retrospect, it seems odd that in the United States so few
angry words were directed at Dame Rumor during the Vietnam War (which may have been a consequence of fighting a
war with no fear of immediate physical danger to this country's
civilian population). Variations on the old refrain from World
War II that "loose lips sink ships" were never uttered during
the Vietnam War. Yet rumors of oppression and deceit did play
an important part. The story of the Mylai massacre of 16 March
1968, which stunned national conscience and outraged world
opinion, persisted in a twilight world of rumor for more than a
year after it happened. Givral, a cafe-cum-patisserie in Saigon,
was famous as the fountainhead of many spicy rumors that surfaced in the world press.

In sharp contrast to this recent period in American history,
feelings against rumormongers ran very high in the United
States during the First and Second World Wars. During World
War I the *New York Times* wrote: "The German agent pervades the land. In every community where he stops overnight
a full-blown rumor pervades the town the next day. It came
from someone on the 'inside', somebody who 'got it straight',
and it is whispered from one to another until the whole community is uneasy and agitated." Citizens were advised by the
Louisville Times: "Every man and woman should become a
detective in the interest of the country, working to lay by the
heels this class of criminals [the rumormongers]." More explicit instructions were provided by the *New York Sun,* which
wrote: "The proper course is to demand precise proof of the
allegations, and if it be not forthcoming, to silence the circulation of evil report by ridicule or by immediate denunciation."
Organizations such as the National Committee of Patriotic
Societies defended America against lies, rumors, and malicious
gossip. Examples of wartime rumors were used to discredit
rumormongers and to create a deviant role for the teller [250].
The same fears were expressed during World War II. It is

contended that the public and the press were given to rumors more than any time previously. There was also concern voiced that a decline in the importance of "truth" might signal a continuing and dangerous trend. [20]. Warnings were again issued about the planting of rumors by Axis agents, and the American public was urged to be especially conscientious in their own communications and judgments of communications by others [31, 162, 164]. Britain made it a legal offense to "publish any report or statement relating to matters connected with the war which is likely to cause alarm or despondency." Cases were tried, particularly at the beginning of the war, when the British situation seemed grim. There was one case in which a headmaster was charged with telling his pupils that the Germans would land in Ireland and blockade Britain, and that the children would have to eat cats and dogs; they might, he added, also get a little rat or snail soup [207].

During World War II, German radio station DEBUNK was a familiar channel for bogie and wedge-driving rumors. Using a combination of news flashes, fake interviews, misquotations, and anecdotes, the chief broadcaster—a man with a slight Virginia accent who called himself Joe Scanlon—attempted to persuade American listeners that prostitution and venereal disease were rampant in U.S. Army camps; that the Allies were in collusion against the United States; that Jews and Negroes were subversives; and that the British were selfishly benefiting from American sacrifices at home [138, 263]. Tokyo Rose, the G.I.s' name for the Japanese equivalent to Joe Scanlon, was in fact an amalgam of Japanese women broadcasters who used similar propaganda devices in an attempt to demoralize U.S. troops stationed in the South Pacific.

Another area of rumor plants is in politics. During the political campaign prior to an election, rumormongering will be especially widespread. A study conducted in India of the 1950–52 general election found that rumors were rampant as election day approached; some tales were planted to create a premature expectation of victory [230].

In the United States the political whispering campaign has a long history [2]. When John Quincy Adams ran against Andrew Jackson, a rumor was started that Jackson and his wife had lived together in adultery. Adams was the target of malicious rumors that he had acted as the pander to a Russian nobleman. When Thomas Jefferson campaigned for the presidency, a whispering campaign was waged by New England clergymen; they started rumors that he was an atheist, that he had debauched a well-born Virginia belle, and that he had sired numerous black children. Martin Van Buren was rumored to be the illegitimate son of Aaron Burr. In the 1972 American presidential campaign, in which Richard Nixon ran against George McGovern, the Republicans were later revealed to have employed "dirty tricksters" to start destructive rumors about leading Democratic presidential hopefuls.

Obviously not all political rumormongering is so calculated as are these examples. Allport and Postman have suggested that the seeds of rumor are planted when the evidence pertaining to an important topic is ambiguous [10]. According to this theory rumors are an attempt to provide structure in an uncertain situation. Thus we might expect that the considerable emotional content and equivocation of campaign addresses is what helps to make presidential politics such a fertile field for wild rumors to take root [43, 117, 219, 220].

Washington, D.C. news correspondent Edward P. Morgan once characterized Dame Rumor as the Capitol's No. 1 Hostess [175]. Morgan described four categories of deliberate political rumors and maintained that their common denominator was "an effort, in one way or another, to stage-manage events, to hatch a situation, and to keep its development under control or prevent the enemy from snatching it away for his own designs." One variety is the self-serving rumor: the eager politician tosses out his own name or a friend's as a promising candidate in order to curry favor or to build up publicity and interest. Another is the appointment rumor to which one-upping Washington hostesses must stay closely attuned. A third is the trial balloon sent up to test public reaction: "If the balloon is not shot down or buffeted by stiff winds of protest it may stay aloft. If resistance is strong, it can be reeled in with a straightforward denial that its ascension was ever intended—or indeed ever made." A fourth category, closely akin to the trial balloon, are leaks which spring up as a result of competitive pressures in governmental agencies.

Like war and politics, there are many other areas where competitiveness and secrecy feed a wellspring of rumor. Reaction to, and anticipation of, the behavior of the stock market is a constant source of rumormongering, although New York Stock Exchange Rule 435 and American Stock Exchange Rule 3c state that the floors of the exchange must be rumor free. As decisions have to be made rapidly if they are to be effective, and as there was usually precious few facts to go on, rumor exerts a significant influence on those who trade in the market [209]. On 6 August 1974, the day after President Richard Nixon confessed to having ordered a halt to F.B.I. investigations of the Watergate break-in and conceded that his impeachment by the House of Representatives was a foregone conclusion, the stock market soared on the first rumors that he might resign; the Dow-Jones climbed more than 25 points in the first half hour. When in 1972 Vietnam peace rumors circulated, the Dow-Jones responded with sudden afternoon spurts. About the same period rumors of U.S.-Soviet "secret gold price deals" boosted the price of gold to new highs on Europe's bullion markets.

It is reported that in some American colleges premedical students spread false information on the morning of an exam in an effort to mislead their unsuspecting peers who are fiercely competing for a limited number of places in medical schools [97]. The secretiveness and competition for priority of discovery in science may also create conditions that are highly conducive to the promulgation of self-serving rumors [cf. 87, 256].

A series of fortuitous events can also serve as an impetus for rumor. When disaster strikes, bogie rumors will proliferate until the danger is well past and tensions are reduced. We mentioned the Wallenpaupack rumor, which was born of unfounded fears about an imagined typhoid epidemic; in other cases realistic warnings have been ignored or greeted with skepticism until issued by an unimpeachable source [65]. It is clear that surprise, shock, and panic are a breeding ground for rumor in time of crisis [60, 145, 154, 196, 197, 229].

We learn that rumors can also occur for benign as well as sinister motives. Not all rumors are deliberate plants. They may not be entirely accidental, but are not methodically intentional in the way that propaganda and persuasion are. These benign rumors start out as opinions and then acquire their "factual" trimmings as they are transmitted. We observe also (Allport and Postman notwithstanding) that ambiguity and importance may not be sufficient to account for the birth and growth of all varieties of rumor—some emotional arousal in the form of anxiety also seems essential. Anxiety due to personality or situational factors, excitement concerning the prospect of a change, or anything unusual that alters the standard cause-and-effect relationship—any or all of these can provide the necessary arousal.

Shibutani's notion of collective problem solving is again appropriate. People base their actions on what sociologist Harold Garfinkel characterizes as the "routine grounds of everyday behavior"—those shared and unstated assumptions that people in a culture make about each other and the world [86]. When things go awry there is an increase in anxiety and a desire to stabilize the situation. One way collective problem solving can occur is through the normal channels of communication. When these break down, alternative means of obtaining information must be sought. Shibutani notes [227, p. 60]: "Spectacular events with possible consequences for millions result in a sudden increase in demand for news that cannot be satisfied even by the most efficient press service."

In some cases information is spread with sufficient rapidity to prevent any substantial rumormongering; in other cases the news simply cannot keep up with the proliferation of rumors. It is clear that the human animal has a desire to know his circumstances, and when the sources from which he receives information are not functioning adequately he will theorize on his own and through acquaintances. Some see this demand for news as being closely related to the level of social excitement [23]. In situations characterized by a high degree of collective excitement, the demand for information will be greater than what can be offered. In situations of low collective excitement, the amount of news is more than ample. This ties in neatly with the social exchange abstraction: news has different values or rewards depending upon supply and demand. The population in a highly agitated frame of mind places a premium on trading useful information.

Some circumstances are structured so the population will be

habitually activated whenever rumors appear—for example, in the Soviet Union where an authoritarian political climate prevents a free flow of reliable information. Bauer and Gleicher interviewed hundreds of Russian emigres to the United States in the late 1940s to discover that word-of-mouth hearsay was critically important to this sample of people who had been unhappy living in the U.S.S.R. [19].

Organizational settings also encourage the activation of rumors when status hierarchies prevent the free flow of information [56]. Those in a position of power exercise control over the kind and amount of information that may be officially released to lower echelons. One study found a prevalence of rumors in an industrial firm where hearsay was frequently related to local economic irregularities pertaining to job security, promotion, benefits, and working conditions [108] (again we observe the implicit role of anxieties). Another study reported systematic rumor flow along a grapevine in a county government department [239].

Thus we find a wide range of motives (and social structures) operating during the birth of a rumor. The same motives will assist in propelling the rumor through the course of its life. Once started, the rumor will continue to travel if conditions are propitious. In the framework of social exchange it can be argued that the optimum conditions occur when there is a mutual compatibility between the motives of the transmitter and the receiver—that is, when the transmitter's needs are satisfied in the telling and the recipient's needs are satisfied in the listening.

STAGE 2—ADVENTURES

The dissemination of rumor can be seen as roughly analogous to the way a complex network of neurons carries information in the human nervous system. Stimulation of the neuron at the receptors is focused onto the stem and then carried to minute nerve endings. At this point there is a gap where the excitation is tranferred to another neuron by chemical interaction. Drugs affect the concentration of transmitter chemicals at the gap and thereby increase or decrease the efficiency of neural transmission. In a similar way, social and psychological "excitations" stimulate the formation of rumors which leap from person to person at a speed that is dependent on the social chemistry. The greater the news value of an event, the more rapid is the process of diffusion [111]. Other "social chemicals" acting as strong moderator variables include the time of day the event occurs or the level of ego-involvement of the audience; these impinge on the level of ar-ousal [70, 71].

The energy used to excite the neuron is nonspecific: the same ion flow occurs whether you hit your finger with a ham-mer, burn it on the stove, or have it bitten by a dog. As long as the excitation is intense, the result will be the same—ignition. It appears also to make little difference in rumormongering the sort of energy used to light the fuse. As long as the need-related "excitation" is sufficiently strong, there will be igni-tion. The dissemination of information cannot match the fan-tastic speed of electrochemical change, although information flow is still quite rapid [76]. When John Kennedy was assassi-nated, nearly 90 percent of the people in this country had word of the shooting within 45 minutes of the first announce-ment [99]. A little more than half the population first heard of the assassination not from the news media, but from another person [111]. Wartime rumors are reported to travel at the same remarkable speed [38].

No psychological rule states that rumormongering, like neural impulses, is a one-way transmission. Indeed it can be argued that rumormongering is actually a two-way channel, since communication is often marked by an exchange of mes-sages (either by another rumor or by a judgment about the one received). Even when looking at two structurally similar ex-amples, communication patterns can vary considerably due to random or idiosyncratic factors. It is theorized that there are conduits (like neural pathways) in which different kinds of in-formation travel, but which can vary depending on the form of the report [59].

During the 1950s, Project Revere at the Public Opinion Laboratory of the University of Washington studied the dis-tribution and effects of airborn messages and other aspects of the dispersion of information [58, 61, 62]. The diffusion of messages on leaflets dropped from planes was greatest when the messages were distributed near closely knit communities and waned with the distance traveled from this type of population center. Small towns appeared to spread information more rapidly than did large cities, and information was frequently shared among friends and acquaintances. Similar patterns were reported for rumors during World War II: the rate and extent of diffusion decreased as the distance from the center of emanation increased, and most of the diffusion occurred through a relatively small number of well-defined paths [38]. The Project Revere researchers also investigated diffusion patterns for other types of information. For instance, they studied the use of chain-tags, by having people send a postcard to the investigators and pass the rest of the postcards to an acquaintance [61]. In this case the most compliance occurred when a strong persuasive appeal was invoked or if the subjects were recompensed (such as in "Earn a Dollar" chain-tags). However, many subjects were uncooperative, particularly if the appeal was too mild.

A similar research strategy was employed by the social psychologist Stanley Milgram in a study he aptly called the small-world problem, which investigated networks of acquaintanceship across the United States [173]. Milgram was inspired by a children's game described by urban planner Jane Jacobs in her book *The Death and Life of Great American Cities* [121]. Jacobs tells how she and her sister would amuse themselves by trying to imagine how they would transport a message via a plausible chain of messengers between two widely disparate geographical points. Milgram adapted the idea for scientific study by having subjects actually move a message across the country using only a chain of friends and acquaintances. The starting point was in Wichita, Kansas or Omaha, Nebraska and the target person was located in Massachusetts. Each person in the chain was instructed to transmit the message to the friend or acquaintance who seemed most likely to know the target person. While not strictly a study in rumor-mongering, the results are illuminating in indicating how few people are needed to transmit information in a purposeful way to a distant point. An average of only five intermediaries was required to move the message to the target person (see FIG. 3). Inspecting the individual chains, Milgram detected a pronounced tendency for women to send the message to women and for men to send it to men.

Rumor diffusion can be conceptualized as a serial chain, in the manner of the information chains in the Milgram studies, or alternately as a contagion, which means a state present in one person will infect another and so on until a whole population has become contaminated [174]. The rumor about the phantom anesthetist of Mattoon is a good example of how a contagion of hysteria can infect an entire population, and many similar examples are noted [40, 140, 154, 224]. Another incident is the pattern of hysterical contagion which accompanied the famous "June bug epidemic," studied by Kerckhoff, Back, and Miller [134, 135]. The outbreak occurred in a small Southern textile factory during the summer of 1962. Over a period of

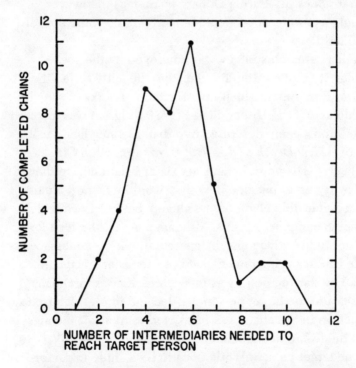

FIGURE 3. The "small world" problem. In the Nebraska study, 2-10 intermediate acquaintances were needed to complete the chain; the median was five. (*After Milgram* [173] *by permission of* Psychology Today Magazine)

one week, 62 people succumbed to an epidemic of imaginary insect bites. The victims, all women, exhibited the classic symptoms of hysteria, and most were physically located within one functional area of the plant. The imaginary bug first "bit" social isolates, but soon the epidemic spread systematically through circles of friends.

One advantage of this contagion metaphor is that it is specific enough for some to construct an analogous mathematical model of the chain reaction when certain conditions are known. Stuart Dodd and his colleages in Project Revere devised mathemical formulas for message diffusion on the basis of exponential or logarithmic functions. Rapoport used the same data to derive more complicated formulas, employing advanced calculus to apply a mathematical theory of random nets to the understanding of informal communication [199, 200, 201]. The contagion metaphor has also been the inspiration for empirical studies which suggest that contagious behaviors are usually mediated by the reduction of group-derived restraints—that is, by the lowering of inhibitions against carrying out an act that personal ideology, group norms, or culture views as under a prohibition or ban [258, cf. 153, 202].

Other models of diffusion embrace certain background features such as the amount of collective excitement in the population and the local predominant cultural mores. To pursue this idea, for example, it may be argued that under conditions of high excitement there is usually a relaxation of conventional norms governing communicative behavior. Thus rumors spread wildly across subgroup and class boundaries without ever being questioned [23]. Emotional needs, attitudes, and values also come into play. Some people are not strongly motivated enough to enter in the grapevine: in studies of organizations it is reported that only a small percentage of employees function as liaisons; most of the rank-and-file are "dead-enders" who hear rumors but never pass them on [55, 240].

The results of an investigation by Festinger, Cartwright et al. demonstrate how emotional needs and values can act as a catalyst for rumormongering [74]. The object of study was a low rent housing project where a rumor had circulated that Communist elements were behind a controversial proposal to establish a nursery school. The main characteristic distinguishing rumormongers from dead-enders is that they participated more routinely in project affairs. The rumormongers were caught up in the activities of the housing project, and due to their greater involvement and need to know, had more information at their finger tips. Being an "insider," with its resultant tension and excitement, apparently intensified the urge to participate in rumormongering.

It is also postulated that the structure of the situation, in particular any effects on the critical orientation of intermediaries, can influence how reliably (or consistently) a rumor is presented [34]. For example, a person highly sensitive to sexual taboos may turn his attention away from stories about sexual depravities or at least be careful to edit any offensive expletives before passing the story on. Alternatively, in circumstances favoring a low critical set, rumors will pass without regard for cultural proprieties; this happens in milling crowds and in groups marked by a sense of what is termed *pseudogemeinschaft* (literally: assumed partnership, or false sense of community).

Distortions, or aberrations, in the substance of a rumor also follow certain patterns [36]. In general they have a tendency to increase in number as the physical distance from the point of emanation increases [145]. They occur whenever there are errors in the encoding, recall, or decoding of the message. Because of the natural porosity of human memory and the tendency to simplify and bring order to things, the most common rumor distortions are the result of leveling (elimination of some details), sharpening (selective attention given to particular information), and assimilation (twisting of new material to build a better overall structure). (See FIG. 4)

The investigation of rumor distortions has taken several forms. An early quasi-experiment in rumor transmission and the study of distortions is that of Thomas Chaloner [cf. 110], a British M.P., whose playful eccentricity was circulated by the 17th century English biographer John Aubrey in *Brief Lives:*

> He had a trick sometimes to goe into Westminster hall in a morning in Terme time, and tell some strange story, and would come thither again about 11 or 12 to have the pleasure to heare how it spred; and sometimes it would be altered, with additions, he could scarce knowe it to be his own.

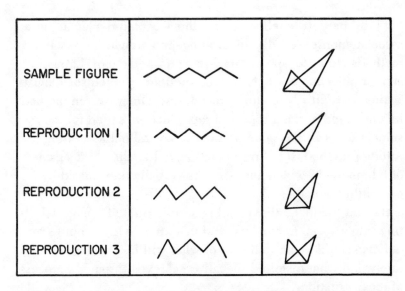

SAMPLE FIGURE		
REPRODUCTION 1		
REPRODUCTION 2		
REPRODUCTION 3		

FIGURE 4. Two sample figures and how they became systematically distorted in successive reproductions. For the zig-zag line, this resulted in a gradual "sharpening" of the points. For the double-peaked polygon, there was a gradual "leveling" of the higher peak. Presumably, analogous patterns of distortion will occur in the serial transmission of a rumor. *(After Wulf [265] as noted in Allport and Postman [10] adapted by permission)*

The psychology of social influence on recall is fundamentally a 20th century concern. Sigmund Freud, in 1901, expounding on the psychopathology of everyday life, included in the scope of his analysis a consideration of the way people forget information as a result of social pressures—motivated forgetting [83]. Freud maintained that forgetting did not occur at random, but was determined by previous events due to repression and other defensive mechanisms of the ego. He did not postulate specific rules of forgetfulness and recall, the implication being that motivated forgetting is idiosyncratic in the main.

The first experimental study of prose recall was conducted by E. H. Henderson at the turn of the century [107]. Subjects were asked to read and recall prose passages of 100–200 words. Henderson discovered that certain regularities occurred—which happen to be very similar to leveling, sharpening, and assimilation.

The major systematic attempt to study the social psychology of recall was the research of the English psychologist, Sir Frederick Bartlett, published in 1932 in his book *Remember-*

ing [18]. Bartlett rebelled against the accepted device of paired associate/nonsense syllable learning, and argued for research methods closer to conventional human interaction. (Lately, a similar objection has been voiced by field-oriented sociologists against Bartlett's laboratory procedures.) One research method he employed, termed repeated reproduction, called for the subject to recall the same passage at several points in time. Another method, serial reproduction, is like the child's game of telephone in which a message is verbally transmitted by one child to another.

Bartlett theorized that recall is most accurate for material fitting into a social framework, and that knowledge of norms and beliefs should be an indicator of what will be recalled accurately and what distorted. Recall is achieved through a process of reconstruction.

When we hear something for the first time, we don't usually have an opportunity or the motivation to memorize it. If we wish to repeat the story some time later, we must employ a "mental schema" involving certain mechanisms in the transformation of material for encoding and recall. These mechanisms were thought to include assimilation, simplification, retention of seemingly unimportant details and social constructiveness. Bartlett used the term assimilation to mean changes in the information during the process of developing cognitive consistency; social constructiveness pertained to additions or major changes not part of the original material, but added to fulfill needs of the person or population.

Numerous studies have been devoted to determining the individual and social variables which affect the retention and forgetting of meaningful material. They reveal the influence of attitudes, beliefs, reference groups, institutions, and other factors. Thus one current theory in psychology states that what is remembered in a given situation depends on the total context of the experience as well as on the demands of the questioner and the knowledge and skill of the person recalling [123]—this contrasts sharply with the old mechanistic view advocating recall as merely the calling forth of associations.

The first halting attempt at scientific experimentation with rumor was by sociologist Clifford Kirkpatrick in 1932. He observed that distortions were frequent when he employed serial reproduction of rumored events [137].

The studies of Gordon Allport and Leo Postman are still the principal experiments on rumor distortion [10]. They attempted to simulate rumormongering by the public performance of serial recall. One standard procedure consisted of projecting a slide depicting a semi-dramatic scene of a large number of related details. Six or seven subjects unfamiliar with the picture waited in an adjacent room. One of the subjects entered and took a position where he could not see the picture, and the experimenter or another subject described the picture giving about 20 details in the account. A second subject entered the room and stood beside the first, who proceeded to tell him all he could about the picture. This "hearsay" account was then communicated to a third subject, and so on. After all the subjects had participated in the rumor chain, the individual accounts were analyzed and contrasted with the picture on the slide. On the basis of these analyses, Allport and Postman postulated the operation of the aforementioned processes involved in distortion (leveling, sharpening, and assimilation). Subsequent research has generally tended to support their conclusions [30, 41, 110, 251, 266].

Thus, in leveling, fewer words are used and fewer details are mentioned as the rumor travels. FIG. 5 shows the number of details retained in successive reproductions of a rumor by word of mouth; the shape of the curve is like the classic Ebbinghaus curve for forgetting as initially there is a sharp decline and then a gradual stabilization. Allport and Postman conclude that social memory accomplishes as much leveling in a few minutes as individual memory accomplishes over weeks [8]. The stabilization of the last part of the curve suggests that a short concise statement is likely to be reproduced faithfully, because the subject has very little detail to select from and the possibilities of further distortion are much less.

In sharpening, which is the reciprocal of leveling, there is an emphasis on a limited number of details from the larger context. Leveling and sharpening cannot exist without each other, for whatever remains of a rumor after leveling has oc-

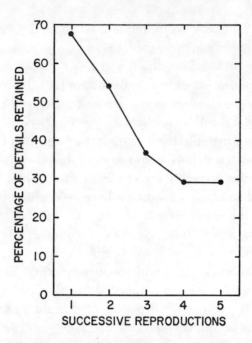

FIGURE 5. The leveling of a rumor. The number of details declined most sharply at the beginning of the serial chain. (*After Allport and Postman* [8] *by permission*)

curred will automatically sharpen. Sharpening of details often occurs when there is a clear implication of movement—for example, something falling or flying or running. Indeed movement may be ascribed to stationary objects merely out of habit. Thus a subway train, clearly at a standstill at a subway station, was frequently described as moving [8]. Relative size is another primary determinant of attention, prominent objects being featured to a greater extent than objects which blended into the background of a picture. Similarly, there was a pronounced tendency to sharpen visual labels (signs, for example) or to emphasize a verbal label which might serve to set the stage for a story ("this is a battle scene" or "this is a race riot"). Sharpening was also provoked by the appearance of familiar symbols or by explanations which provided closure to a story.

In assimilation we find the psychological process which may mediate both leveling and sharpening. Habits, interests, and sentiments exert a powerful force on a rumor which pushes it in a particular direction. Thus it generally happens that items become assimilated in the principal theme in order to make a better Gestalt, or there may be an attempt to complete incompleted pictures or to fill in gaps ("good continuation"). Sometimes there is assimilation by condensation: it is easier to remember one item than two, and therefore some summary phrase is perpetuated in successive accounts of the story. Expectations and linguistic habits can also produce assimilative distortions, as when stereotyped images are invoked. However, the essential process is one of reducing stimuli to a simple and meaningful structure that has adaptive significance for the individual in terms of his own interests and experience [8].

It is not entirely clear to what extent the distortions of communication are due to distorted perceptions as opposed to selective forgetting and repression. Psychologists note that various factors in one's frame of reference can shape the observer's eye [226]. We judge words and deeds with the aid of reference points that provide a standard of comparison. In a crisis these psychological anchors may no longer be relevant or operational. Without any new standards to judge or to verify, credulity stretches to encompass distorted perceptions that irrationally support rumors. A study conducted in 1950 of a natural castastrophe in India found cases of distorted perceptions strengthening and corroborating hearsay; one report had it that Mt. Everest significantly changed shape [229].

Leveling, sharpening, and assimilation are just three of many possible kinds of biases and variations [36]. There is also the tendency to be silent about unpleasant news to avoid the negative reaction which greets the bearer of bad tidings [160, 210]. How strong this tendency is could depend on the degree of candor and credibility of formal news sources; when news is scarce or when official channels are closed or unreliable, there is a high reliance on word-of-mouth communication for both bad and good news [19].

In discussing the Paul McCartney rumor we alluded to another variation of assimilative distortions when we mentioned the integration of oddities discovered on old album covers and in recordings. This attempt to bring order to things by introducing new meaning to events insignificant before the rumor appeared is known as cognitive reorganization [74]. Still another factor producing distortions is an ambiguity in the use of terms [157]. The meaning of a report is easily altered when a word or phrase is misunderstood. Former Presidential press secretary Ronald L. Ziegler, when questioned about the obfuscation that goes on in briefing reporters about White House happenings, explained the lack of candor during the Nixon Administration as a bureaucratic "habit pattern" [178]. Therefore, ambiguity and equivocation may be synonymous with power and persuasion in the minds of many politicians, because commitments can be avoided which might antagonize or alienate some segment of the voting population.

Thus the needs and habits of intermediaries can significantly shape the construction of messages they share. If the need for power be served by clever political phrases, candor will become a scarce commodity.

STAGE 3 - DEATH

Intermediaries in the chain of communication can play an active or passive role in the dissemination of rumor. Wishful thinking or a deliberate need to influence can distort or bias a tale. Alternatively, the second person may be a dead-ender or he may play a passive liaison role and transmit the story intact. The same levels of motivational activity will operate in the final stage of the rumor cycle. Some stories die a natural death because people have grown weary of the issue and have stopped talking or thinking about it. Rumors also expire when underlying tensions have dissipated. In the rumor about the phantom anesthetist of Mattoon, there was a close relationship between the dissipation of hysteria and "recoveries" of his victims [124]. However, there may also be a vigorous counteroffensive, as in the rumor in Orléans; the tide began to turn against the whisperers only after a concerted battle was fought between them and the print media [176]. Some rumors are still-born; others never reach maturity as gauged by popular belief or knowledge.

How a rumor dies depends on the nature of the tale within the social context. Some rumors never die, but become part of the established popular belief structure. Thomas Carlyle once characterized history as "a distillation of rumour." Some rumors become so deeply enmeshed in the web of recorded history that they cannot easily be excised [191]. John Kennedy's assassination produced a spate of rumors, many still alive in the hearts and minds of those disinclined to believe the findings of the Warren Commission. Leaving aside the justification of these rumors, it is not unreasonable to forecast that a hundred years from now stories will still be circulating about that fateful November day. Rumors in the dormant stage on occasion have reactivated. In the aftermath of Watergate and subsequent disclosures of other illegal and unethical clandestine activities of the F.B.I. and C.I.A., much of what once was casually dismissed as impossible or improbable became the subject of renewed interest and plausible speculation.

Myths and legends are defined by this same enduring quality. The Paul McCartney episode has been compared to the legend of the Greek god Dionysus, who was rumored to have suffered a violent death and then been resurrected [238]. Another parallel is that some of the more devoted followers used hallucinogens and other drugs to escape from dull reality and the banality of existence.

More recently the specter of the legendary "flying Dutchman"—the mythical sailor sentenced to pilot his ship until Judgment Day—has reappeared in the form of a modern-day rumor about haunted jetliners. The story goes that the faces of the pilot and crew of an Eastern Airlines Tristar that crashed in the Florida Everglades in December 1972 have mysteriously reappeared in the cockpits of other Tristars. Some pilots and stewardesses have been so badly frightened that they have refused to fly the "haunted" jetliner. According to an account in the *New York Times* (April 13, 1975) airline officials went to great lengths to track down the elusive source of the rumor, but to no avail. Assuming that the age of interplanetary travel is nearer at hand than the Day of Judgment, rumors of haunted rocketships in newspapers of the future are not beyond the realm of possibility.

Monster buffs, quick to rush into sensational claims based on the most flimsy evidence, have for centuries preserved from extinction wild fictions about sea monsters, devil babies, unicorns, and other fantastic mythical creatures [45]. The rumor of the devil-baby is an especially persistent tale. Jane Addams, one of the early leaders in the social work movement and the founder in 1889 of the Chicago settlement house known as Hull House, described the resurrection in rumor of the devil-baby legend [3, pp. 117–118]:

> We had a remarkable experience at Hull House this year of the persistence of one of these tales which has doubtless had its taming effects through the centuries upon recalcitrant husbands and fathers. It burst upon us one day in the persons of three Italian women who, with an excited rush into Hull House, demanded to see the devil-baby. No amount of denial convinced them that it was not there, for they knew exactly what it was like, with its cloven hoofs, its pointed ears, and its diminutive tail. It had been able to speak as soon as it was born and was most shockingly profane. For six weeks the messages, the streams of visitors from every part of the city and suburbs to this mythical baby, poured in all day long and so far into the night that the regular activities were almost swamped. The Italian version, with a hundred variations, dealt with a pious Italian girl married to an athiest who vehemently tore a holy picture from the bedroom wall, saying that he would quite as soon have a devil in the house as that, whereupon the devil incarnated himself in the child. As soon as the devil-baby was born, it ran about the table shaking its finger in deep reproach at its father, who finally caught it and in fear and trembling brought it to Hull House. When the residents there, in spite of the baby's shocking appearance, in order to save its soul took him to the church for baptism, they found the shawl was empty, and the devil-baby, fleeing from the holy water ran lightly over the back of the pews.

Although rumors born of myth have the potential for rebirth, the average rumor, once activated or reborn, has a relatively brief life span. The active life of the Paul McCartney rumor lasted only a few months [214]. The rumor in Orléans, in which innocent Jewish shopkeepers were vilified as white slavers, died out after two months [176]. The tale of the phantom anesthetist of Mattoon persisted for about a fortnight [124]. Most rumors are born, have a period of prominence, and then disappear [213]. This disappearance usually takes one of three forms—disproof, irrelevance, or dissipation.

In the first instance, disproof, the story is denied in order to end it as quickly as possible. Rumors about disasters are often stopped by prompt denial from a credible source. This is true in the case of the Wallenpaupack rumor, which was effectively quashed when trusted river officials denied on the radio that the dam had broken and offered a plausible genesis to the fiction [54]. The rumor in Orléans was killed by newspapers that exposed logical contradictions in the kidnapping story [176]. There are also institutional mechanisms, such as radio and television open-lines, newspaper columns, censorship, and rumor control centers to disprove fallacious stories at their outset.

In the late 1960s rumor control centers sprouted across the United States to function as social controls. Similar services have operated as a response to the civil disorders in Northern Ireland; in England there exists a federation of several hundred Citizens' Advice Bureaux that are oriented to noncrisis times but work the same as rumor control centers in the U.S. [193]. The centers in the U.S. can be traced to the rumor clinics of World War II. One of these was the Syracuse University Rumor Clinic, which published a weekly newspaper column analyzing and refuting rumors. Research conducted at the time revealed that followers of the column tended to believe less in wartime rumors than did occasional readers [5], although it was uncertain whether this was an inoculation effect attributable to the power of the press or a difference due to the possibility that a more thoughtful reader was drawn to the column.

Experience teaches that prompt, unequivocal disproof is the most effective way of stopping a rumor. Disproving a false rumor at its onset, before people have had time to conclude that the story is "true" and that others have a personal stake in hiding the facts, attacks the problem before the rumor can establish itself. It is essential to present the facts as fully as possible in order to quell idle speculations. A key factor, at least initially, is the audience's trust in the source of the information. Psychologist Elliott McGinnies conjectures that rumormongers and gossips, because of the so-called "sleeper effect," may have a pernicious influence that persists long after the source of the information has been discredited [163]. The sleeper effect (a subject of some controversy lately; cf. 48, 91) was first studied by social psychologists Carl I. Hovland and Walter Weiss at Yale University in an experiment which contrasted the impact of communications attributable either to a high or a low credibility source [116]. When the audience was tested immediately after the communication, those for whom the source was represented as highly credible showed greater positive attitude gains in the advocated direction that those for whom the source was low in credibility. However, one month later a delayed, or sleeper, effect set in: agreement with the untrustworthy sources had increased whereas agreement with the trustworthy sources had decreased (see FIG. 6). Hovland and Weiss explained this phenomenon as a tendency over a period of time to disassociate the source of the message from its content, the implication being that a person rejects a story from an untrustworthy source at the moment he first hears it, but shows a delayed acceptance when he has forgotten the source. Other research suggests that the less open a belief system, the more difficult to act upon information for its own merits and apart from the positive or negative characteristics of the source [195].

Once opinions start to form, it becomes increasingly difficult to put an end to them. Like prejudices, hardening with time, the more established and rehearsed the opinion the less vul-

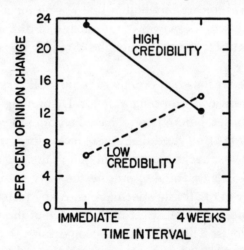

FIGURE 6. A diagram of the "sleeper effect," showing the net per cent change in opinions over a time interval of four weeks. (After Hovland and Weiss [116] by permission of the second author and The Public Opinion Quarterly)

nerable it is to counterargument [165, 212]. We mentioned the boomerang effect when *Life* magazine attempted to refute the false rumor of Paul McCartney's death. This merely added fuel to the story, which was otherwise on the verge of dying out. Recall also the rumor in Detroit about the little boy having been castrated. The attempted disproof of this story ironically became its verification. When a local newspaper denied the incident, the effort backfired and the tale spread further as some rumormongers began to cite the published account as their source of information [211].

It is not always a simple matter to decide what procedure will be the most effective in disproving a rumor. A method that is adequate in denying one story may not work for another. Shibutani alludes to this dilemma in noting a Government campaign in the 1940s to combat rumors of supposedly treasonous actions conducted by local Japanese-Americans in the attack on Pearl Harbor [227]. Stories of illegal activities continued despite denials by the Honolulu Chief-of-Police, the Director of the F.B.I., and the U.S. Secretary of War. Shibutani suggests that the resistance to denial was not due to any deep-seated lack of faith in these sources, but to the belief that the rules of censorship forced them to lie to protect national security interests in time of war. A similar phenomenon was reported during World War II: official campaigns against rumors occasionally backfired and caused an increase in rumormongering because they enhanced the value of the forbidden information [38].

In the Wallenpaupack episode, to prevent a boomerang effect from occurring, official radio reports were carefully edited to forestall any possibility that someone might tune in on the news message only long enough to hear the word "dam" and then panic and run [54]. The first official report stated: "Ladies and gentlemen, the rumor that has been going around that the Wallenpaupack Dam broke is not true; it is nothing but a rumor. We have been in contact with Dam officials." However, the final edited version eliminated all references to dam, water, or flood: "Ladies and gentlemen. It is only a rumor—it is *not* true. There is no need for anyone to be up on mountains or high places. It would be best if you returned home and did not spread the rumor." Even under these circumstances substantially fewer people believed the denial after hearing it from one source than believed the rumor initially.

A rumor will also disappear if it becomes irrelevant. Some tales fade away because they become unresponsive to the needs of their rumor public. This is true for rumors that are essentially predictive. Once the event has occurred and the facts are known, the rumor becomes superfluous. This is certainly true in rumors of election results and political incidents [230] (unless the tales are resurrected to serve some new political purpose). When the emotional tenor of the times changes, the effect of the rumor in satisfying old needs will also dissolve. Returning to the castration rumor that circulated in Detroit with Dr. Martin Luther King Jr.'s death—this fear rumor could no longer be sustained by racial animosities. The climate of hate now changed to one of sadness and sympathy [211]. Rumors are born within a certain emotional climate; they become irrelevant when this period has passed and they no longer serve their original purpose.

Although a particular tale may no longer be current, the grapevine can still survive and function very well. Keith Davis has studied grapevines in organizational settings and observed their fickle, dynamic nature. Rumormongering is a natural social interaction, he argues, and suppressing it in one place may only cause it to appear somewhere else [57]. Nonetheless, a major outbreak of rumors can be a devastating affair, and experience teaches that the specific stories should be dealt with firmly and consistently.

The third case in which rumors disappear is where the story dies a natural death or just fades away. Rumors, particularly those having no personal effect upon their public, die because people grow tired of an issue and shift their attention to other matters. Boredom and frustration can stop a rumor. Shibutani notes that problem solving rumors will dissipate when interests are drawn to other news events [227]. The rumor about Paul McCartney may have dissolved for this reason; the events were not directly relevant for subjects, new information became scarce, and there was not much prestige in retelling the same old story. Because the exchange value lessened with each retelling, the law of diminishing returns took over [214].

Emotional rumors can also disintegrate. Hysterical contagion subsides after a while, as do rumors of hate and fear [25]. These rumors are closely related to fads and crazes in their spread and subsequent exhaustion. Rumors that are not of sufficient importance to be dealt with, and are not of a predictive nature, will eventually expire from overexposure and undernourishment.

While the life cycle of a rumor is predictable within certain limits, its rhythm is a function of a complex social chemistry whose structural regularities are not always apparent. In order to identify the principal components of this process we must search for common elements in the different levels of abstraction.

four : : Perspectives on Rumor

[When] competent observers advocate
strongly divergent points of view, it
seems likely on a priori grounds that
both have observed something valid
about the natural situation, and that
both represent a part of the truth.

D. T. CAMPBELL AND J. C. STANLEY
*Experimental and Quasi-Experimental
Designs for Research*

Psychologists and sociologists who study rumor advocate different views regarding both function and form. Psychologists emphasize individual needs and the serial transmission of hearsay. Sociologists stress collective actions and complex interbehavioral networks. Between these two extremes other theories and hypotheses exist, in a domain drawn from aspects of both. The levels of abstraction represented in these hypotheses are not in opposition to one another in any fundamental sense; each discipline lays claim to a different stratum of human behavior and emotion and together they form the continuum from which contemporary social psychology is a hybrid offshoot.

PSYCHOLOGISTS ON RUMORS

Theoretical work by psychologists on the function of rumor conforms to a kind of "medical model" presupposing that rumors are the expression of individual states of mind, much as disease symptoms are basically individual physical manifestations. Certainly the most widely cited psychological theory of rumor is that of Gordon Allport and Leo Postman deriving from the Gestalt assertion that perceptions strive toward simplicity, order, and a feeling of closure [8, 9, 10].

Allport and Postman

Allport and Postman postulate that importance and ambiguity are the key ingredients in rumormongering. Human beings are motivated to make sense of their environment; there is an "effort after meaning." Our minds strive to eliminate chaos and uncertainty. When the truth is not directly forthcoming we piece together information as best we can, giving rise to rumors, rationalizations, and the search for a definition of the situation. The reason rumors circulate is that they explain things and relieve the tensions of uncertainty.

Earlier it was noted that several models for the process of rumor spread have been developed at various levels of mathematical sophistication. Allport and Postman's is an exemplar of simplicity: to wit, $R = i \times a$. The formula translates as [10, pp. 61–62]: "rumors (R) concerning a given subject-matter will circulate within a group in proportion to the importance (i) and the ambiguity (a) of this subject-matter in the lives of individual members of the group."

This emphasis on the variable of ambiguity has compelling empirical support in its favor, which is detailed in the next chapter. However, with the exception of the intuitive appeal given by the equal stress laid on the importance variable, the significance of this second variable has never actually been demonstrated. (In the next chapter we discuss research which uncovered a puzzling, inverse relationship between the perceived importance of subject matter and the rate of rumormongering in an ambiguous situation.)

It is argued by Chorus that the inverse of critical sensibility $1/c$ also be included as a multiplicative variable in the Allport and Postman formula [42]; that is: $R = i \times a \times 1/c$. As critical sensibility increases, rumormongering weakens and eventually stops, while someone with low critical sensibility is a likely candidate for rumormongering because he accepts everything uncritically. The multiplication sign informs us that this is postulated as an all-or-none relationship: if the subject matter is unimportant or unambiguous (or if critical sensibility is extremely high) then rumormongering is nil. Of course, situations completely devoid of ambiguity are rare; likewise, all aspects of life have some degree of importance for a sentient and active human being even to a minimal degree. Still there is a strong intuitive appeal to this formula: disasters and other crises are characterized by high importance, high ambiguity, low critical sensibility, and many rumors.

While not as well known as Allport and Postman's theory, other psychological work conforming to the "medical" analogy provides illuminating insights into the possible functions of rumormongering. All this work assumes that though society consists of individuals interacting in a collectivity, the individual bases of social phenomena must also be stressed. Because individuals transmit and respond to rumor, rumor must in some way serve individual needs. That rumormongering is commonplace suggests that needs must be widespread. As similar rumors appear in different cultures at different times indicates that the needs might be universal.

Jung

The psychoanalytic theory of rumor propounded by Carl J. Jung proceeds from such assumptions [126, 127, 128]. Jung argues that for the dissemination of an "ordinary" rumor nothing more is required than "popular curiosity and sensation-mongering." Rumors give vent and expression to anxieties and hostilities. (We know also that rumors can be a catalyst, if not actually a source, of fears and apprehensions.) In the language of psychoanalysis, rumormongering is a defense-mechanism. It soothes the ego by relieving the uncomfortable pressures of excessive anxiety. This is accomplished by the process of projection: anxieties are converted into lesser threats by attributing unacceptable desires or feelings that are actually one's own to outside forces.

By way of illustrating this principle, Jung analyzed a schoolroom rumor among young girls based on the semi-erotic dream of one of the girls. The dream and the rumor expressed the ambivalent love-hate relationship between the student and her male instructor. In Jung's words [127, pp. 188–189]: ". . . the dream formed the first expression for something that was already in the air; it was the spark which fell into the powder magazine."

Festinger

Leon Festinger, in his well-known cognitive dissonance theory, has also speculated on the ego-defensive function of rumor [73]. The theory asserts that dissonance will exist between two ideas (or cognitions) when the opposite of one follows from the other. For instance, two dissonant cognitions would be:

(a) I detest rumormongers,
(b) I like to hear a juicy rumor.

The dissonance produced by these discrepant ideas functions similar to any other drive. If we are hungry, we do something to reduce our discomfort from the hunger; if we experience cognitive dissonance, we do something to reduce our discomfort from it.

The inspiration for cognitive dissonance theory was in Festinger's own attempt to reconcile an intriguing discrepancy in the reported behavior of local inhabitants after a major earthquake in India. In contrast to the hedonistic assumption that people will put unpleasant things out of their minds, there was a constant flow of rumors predicting calamities; and these exaggerated expectations of destruction and disaster predominated in the regions that had been least affected by the earthquake. Festinger explained the rumors as attempts to reconcile dissonant cognitions. People in the untouched regions were afraid, but having no concrete grounds for their fears, manufactured reasons in order to reduce the psychological discomfort resulting in holding two contrary ideas (that is, they were unharmed but still felt anxious and apprehensive).

SOCIOLOGISTS ON RUMORS

Aside from any functions that rumors and rumormongering have for individuals, they also have a social function and serve needs of the collectivity. Indeed, individual and collective needs are sometimes opposed: wartime rationing programs serve the collective need but not the commodity needs of individual citizens. At this more "molar" level of analysis further assumptions about the nature of the rumor public are made which may be valid only in certain circumstances. First, it is usually assumed that rumors spread in clusters or are discussed by the collectivity. This derives from the belief that the primary determining factor in a spreading rumor is consensus, which is only feasible when a group hears the rumor and gives a reasonably rapid chain of feedback. (No doubt the presence of leaders or other higher status individuals help the consensus develop with alacrity.) Second, it is usually assumed that the group shares common concerns and that there is the possibility of consensus. Recent investigation shows that once a group has arrived at a position favored by the majority, a bandwagon effect can develop fairly quickly [93]. Hence, one who sits quietly by while opinions are initially being sorted out may discover that the time has passed when a new opinion can make a difference to the consensus. However, bogie and pipe dream rumors can crystalize differences, and wedge-driving rumors can split groups apart. Thus it is perhaps the exceptional rumor or informational report in which the entire society is included. Even in those cases, certain exceptional individuals (the exceptionally infirm, unstable, or immature) may be shielded from the reports to which everyone else is privy.

Shibutani

The premier work in this area is *Improvised News,*
published in 1966 by Tamotsu Shibutani. The thesis of the
book is expressed as follows [227, p. 164]: "Rumor is a collective transaction whose component parts consist of cognitive
and communicative activity; it develops as men caught together in an ambiguous situation attempt to construct a meaningful interpretation of it by pooling their intellectual resources." Shibutani sees something akin to natural selection
operating—the survival of the fittest rumor. As the group
strives for consensus, they eliminate those rumors that are
least satisfactory or plausible in terms of the contingencies of
behavior accepted by the group.

Expressed in more general terms, the argument is that
societies—being always in flux—give rise to crises whenever
some new event cannot be understood on the basis of established assumptions. When existing expectations are violated,
new sensitivities and new ideas emerge. For people to act in
concert they must alter their orientations together, which can
be accomplished by comparing impressions. Hence, rumormongering is a problem solving transaction in which a form of
collective critical ability is operating. It is a means of adapting
to change, and it facilitates social control when the existing
order is believed to be in jeopardy [cf. 109, 198].

An example of this is a crime of passion whose immediate
aftermath we chanced to witness. A murder was committed in
the old Society Hill section of Philadelphia, Pennsylvania on a
Sunday afternoon in late August 1971. The victim was a locally
prominent police surgeon. His killer, a 32 year old female
psychiatric aide, believed him to be professionally envious of
and hostile to her roommate, a practicing psychiatrist. Pos-
sessed with this idea the killer confronted her victim in a park-
ing lot outside a high-rise apartment complex and shot him
three times at close range. Residents and passersby converged
on the scene, and a steady ebb and flow of questions and
speculations began on the who, what, and why of the murder.

Rumors proliferated, each new theory attempting to reach consensus. At one point a sportscar squealed wheels as it suddenly accelerated and sped around a nearby corner. Someone joked that the driver must be trying to escape from the scene of the crime—the remark was instantaneously picked up by a portion of the crowd and was for a minute part of the collectively sanctioned conception of the incident. Minutes later the killer surrendered, but until her identity became known, the feeling that it was a random urban crime in which anyone present might have been murdered, fed the ambiguity and apprehension at the core of the rumormongering.

Turner and Killian, Roos, and Jung

There is another, more ephemeral quality to this communication process by which a loosely bound collectivity arrives at a collectively sanctioned solution to a problem. Turner and Killian, among others, point out that rumors can serve to validate a course of action (for example, the rumors that always precede a riot) or to confirm or express a commonly shared image or mood so intense that it requires validation in some collective attitude or action [252]. In an accident or crime there is a back and forth shuttling of questions and speculations which provide collective closure to the situation [119, 179]. The solitary individual caught in a crisis is anxious and restless, and actively engages in restructuring activities aimed at finding out what will happen next. The "verbal milling" of individuals in a crisis resembles the restless, agitated state in the milling of cattle when a summer storm is brewing. To sociologists like Turner and Killian, milling is a communication process, and rumor is milling in its basically verbal form.

Roos has also alluded to this essentially unconscious force of collective behavior in interpreting the scuttlebutt he heard aboard a U.S. troopship during World War II [208]. He writes: "Hidden under the cloak of fatalistic acceptance was always the fantasy that 'nothing is going to happen to me; if anything does occur, it will be the next fellow, and not myself, whose number is up.'" In this way pipe dream rumors are tailor-made to suit the individual needs of all, yet they serve the collective wish of destroying a common enemy without dwelling on the perception of an individual peril.

Carl Jung's theory of ordinary rumors was stated in terms of individual needs and ego-defensive reactions. Jung also discusses a variation of the ordinary rumor, which he characterizes as an expression in the form of a vision—hence, the term "visionary rumor" [128]. In this case, collective rather than individual needs are stressed. The primary requisite for a visionary rumor is an unusual emotion which possesses a stronger degree of excitation than do ordinary rumors. Such emotions, Jung argues, reside in age-old ideas (or archetypes) which are an inherent part of the collective unconscious, the personality's cultural heritage. Thus the primitive archetype of innocent death, an idea culturally transmitted from generation to generation, is a recurrent theme in folklore and legend; it provides, for example, a psychoanalytic interpretation for the McCartney rumor [238]. Rumors of flying saucers are also seen as projections of an archetypal image. The emotional basis for them is thought to be the distress that results from collective fear and anxiety over the world situation and the universal wish for a redeeming supernatural force. The flying saucer rumor is therefore a recurrent theme: in the 16th century there were reports of "globes" and "tubes" seen in the air moving with great speed and sometimes appearing to turn upon each other as if fighting. Because this rumor is a "psychic manifestation" it appears as well in the content of dreams. (The recurrence of rumors in wartime of mass poisoning and rape is explained by Loewenberg in a similar way, as a projection of a primitive archetypal image [154].)

OTHER VIEWS ON RUMORS

Other theoretical work on rumor is not easily pigeonholed into the psychological or sociological compartment, but draws from aspects of both.

Knopf (Contextual Elements)

Terry Ann Knopf, in her recent book entitled *Rumors, Race and Riots,* has presented a promising eclectic interpretation of

rumors associated with racial rioting in the United States [141].
She postulates what is termed a process-model of rumor, emphasizing a functional basis with certain contextual features in
the sociological vein. The core of racial rumors, she contends,
is the animosity between blacks and whites. For white people,
blacks are perceived as the cause of trouble; for black people,
whites are the cause. This mutual misperception resulting in
animosity is the crucial element in the promulgation of racial
rumors, serving to identify the specific sources of strain for the
individual rumormonger and assigning responsibility accord-
ingly. In the riot of 1965 in Watts, a black residential area of
Los Angeles, rumors about police brutality were invoked as an
explanation for the episode. The opinion widely held was
police considered black people criminals and tramps; stories
were told about policemen striking pregnant women and beat-
ing old women [174, p. 574]. Knopf points out that these kinds
of rumors serve multiple functions: they crystallize the hostile
ideas held by each side; they confirm hostility as "fact"; and
they intensify the underlying emotions. The social structure,
the political climate, and opportunities available for the
emergence of a certain rumor—all are contextual features
which assist in determining rumor themes. The Watts' rumors
were presumably a reflection of anti-police sentiment as well
as the belief that the police and white people in general were
the cause of trouble for blacks.

Knopf conceptualizes rumormongering within the general
social framework. How we perceive the meaning of experience
also derives in large part from the total existential context
[cf. 23]. Strands woven into the fabric of society have patterns and colorations which influence our cast of mind. One
obvious element is the sociopolitical climate. Professor Mark
Harris has attributed the rash of conspiracy rumors proliferat-
ing during the post-Watergate period of 1975 to a pervasive
atmosphere of mistrust and suspicion nurtured by startling
realities [103, p. 12]:

The United States Government breaks into the office of Daniel
Ellsberg's psychiatrist in the name of national security. But it was
the doctor's patient who had brought the Pentagon Papers to light,

providing support in detail for the war scandal that the left theorists of conspiracy had intuited. So who was really crazy? . . . we have ascended to the highest levels of the suspension of disbelief. Where so much has been established as true, little exists that we who are filled with love of orderly process can outright deny. Myth and invention pass for fact.

Proximity and relevance provide other contextual strands whose subtleties and details determine the patterns and pathways of rumor. Thus we know that rumors will spread most quickly in the area where they started; the rate of diffusion should decrease in some rough ratio to the distance from the point of emanation [38]. Rumors also tend to spread in networks seemingly adapted for this purpose [57, 59, 239]—for example, the organizational grapevine. Rumors spread to persons for whom the content is most relevant [74, cf. 27, 146]. Thus rumors of racial violence will spread among those with racial fears or hates; rumors about politicians or rock musicians will spread among those most intrigued by these subcultures; rumors about military maneuvers will spread among those with strongly partisan sympathies.

Buckhout and Hart

Research on certain aspects of legal testimony which involves a verbal interaction between lawyer and witness concerning the perceptions of an event, falls within this sphere of inquiry. As every lawyer knows, reports of witnesses are usually less than totally accurate, even when they strain their ability to reproduce a story as faithful to reality as possible. We do not often have access to a taped recording of a crime; when we do, or when we plan one ourselves, inaccuracies abound in spectators' reports. Social science professors routinely warn students about trusting their recall of first impressions.

Psychologist Robert Buckhout conducted an experiment on eyewitness testimony in which he videotaped a staged assault on a college professor in front of 141 eyewitnesses [33]. After the attack Buckhout took sworn testimony from each witness to compare what they thought they observed with what actually occurred. Descriptions of the assailant were quite inaccurate;

and six weeks later, when the witnesses were asked to identify him from a set of six photographs, the error rate was very high. In the courtroom, however, the eyewitness is naively presumed to have a perfectly accurate and indellible impression of the crime (like a human videotape machine). Buckhout, and others [259], note that the distortions occurring in testimony closely parallel those in rumor transmission.

Writing in 1916, Dr. Bernard Hart, a psychiatrist, argued that the key to understanding a rumor is found in the elements operating during the person-to-person transmission of a report [104]. A story passing from one person to another will change—not entirely due to willful manipulation of the transmitter but to unconscious forces and elements in the process itself. Hart identified two factors in particular: "perversions" and the "herd instinct." Perversions are distortions in communication (as in the perversion of legal testimony). Hart believed that there are three mechanisms involved in the perversion of evidence: selective attention, which causes us to pick out from material presented by our senses only that which interests us; selective recall, in which we repress emotionally threatening material and overemphasize what is most satisfying to our senses; the suggestive power of the questions we are asked. The cohesive ingredient in the operation of these three is the "psychic complexes" which define and influence the human personality.

The other basic factor postulated was the instinctive behavior of the herd to close ranks—in the broadest sense a species survival mechanism [cf. 171]. In applying this Freudian concept to an understanding of rumor, Hart characterized it as that unconscious force of civilization which directs the individual to be in harmony with his fellow man. The herd instinct was seen as a fundamental fact of human nature, minimized in the sphere of rational thinking but nonetheless a potentially powerful determinant of opinions and beliefs. When the herd instinct summons, this irresistible urge overwhelms the rational mind. Absurd tales, which otherwise would be immediately rejected, become plausible and contagious rumors. This idea persists in modern social psychology, although the term "herd instinct" is no longer popular. Festinger's social comparison hypothesis argues that there is a need to evaluate one's opinions and beliefs in order to see if they measure up to the standards of one's peer group. As with the herd instinct, the basic drive in social comparison is the wish to be in harmony with others [72].

Like Hart, Buckhout lists factors which appear to limit one's ability to give a complete account of witnessed events. First there are situational determinants: the immediate significance of the episode, how long it was observed, the physical environment. Second is the unreliability of human perception, usually sloppy and inexact and which may be made more so by biological limitations or by the observer's emotional state or expectancies. Third is the tendency to fill in some details (see FIG. 7). Fourth are psychological pressures for conformity, which can slant the observer's vision and judgment. Most of these are familiar ideas from the discussion in chapter 3, and constitute a kind of eclectic view

RESUMÉ

Thus far we have surveyed a wide range of observations concerning the nature of rumor. Sociologists contend that rumormongering is used to validate or to crystallize a commonly shared belief, image, or mood by associating it with a

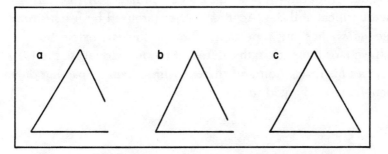

FIGURE 7. "Filling in" of details occurred when observers were shown an incomplete but roughly triangular figure and immediately afterward were asked to draw what they had seen. The typical drawing was a good reproduction of the original (a). A month later, observers asked to draw what they remembered produced more regular figures (b). Three months after the original viewing, again asked to draw what they remembered, they drew erroneously complete, symmetrical figures (c). (After Buckhout [33] by permission of Scientific American, Inc.)

course of action. They interpret rumormongering as a collective, problem solving adaptation to social change when the existing order is in jeopardy. Psychologists emphasize some of these same functions but others as well: rumors are an effort to provide meaning as human beings strive to make sense of their environment; rumors give vent and expression to anxieties and hostilities; rumors provide a means for reconciling dissonant beliefs.

The notion of rumor as a transaction mediated by anxiety reduction is common to all these interpretations and is also consistent with various observations in regard to the evolution and disintegration of rumor (as discussed in chapter 3). Although the result is not always successful, rumor strives to reduce stresses and anxieties. For the individual who believes the rumor due to personal needs, for the transmitter who unwittingly distorts it, for groups of individuals who pass a story along definite pathways, and for cultures which use hearsay to arrive at consensus or to eliminate instability—all of these are a means of mediating anxiety from the individual to the societal level. Anxiety, whether it be overt or inherent in the social situation, appears highly conducive to rumormongering and information exchange, possibly because it intensifies the individual's discomfort when he is confronted by ambiguity and uncertainty. It is also possible that anxiety distorts his evaluation of the evidence in a given situation by interfering with critical abilities. Acute anxieties (aroused by fears, strong needs, wishes and expectancies) might to some extent be allayed, or their strength diluted, if the individual is able to spread his discomfort and share it with others by passing on an emotionally charged rumor.

five : : Some Logical Inferences

It seems that the human mind has
first to construct forms independently
before we can find them in things.

ALBERT EINSTEIN
Main Weltbild

To begin testing the strands which tie our earlier ideas together, let us consider the variables of anxiety and ambiguity
in the light of evidence derived from experiments on rumor.
Inspired by Gestalt psychology, Allport and Postman postulated that the amount of rumor in circulation should vary with
the ambiguity of evidence pertaining to the issue involved.
Shibutani emphasized the variable of ambiguity: rumors develop as people caught in an ambiguous situation attempt to
interpret it by pooling what they have heard. There are only a
few empirical studies that have examined the function of anxiety and ambiguity as independent variables in rumormongering, but with the direct evidence they provide, we can begin
to forge a chain of probable inference.

Experiments on Rumor

The first successful attempt to manipulate ambiguity as a prime factor in determining the intensity of rumormongering was made by the social psychologists, Stanley Schachter and Harvey Burdick [221]. Other research had planted rumors, but had obtained only meagre effects. In these studies the average proportion of the population hearing the planted rumor ranged from zero to only 6 percent, and the average number that reported having spread a rumor was only 0–4 percent of the total sample [16, 75, 222]. These low percentages precluded any possibility of uncovering substantial differences between groups, a fact which inspired Schachter and Burdick to try a quite different, surreptitious type of manipulation using confederates to lay the groundwork for potential rumormongering.

The Schachter and Burdick Experiment

This study took place in a girls' preparatory school. There were three manipulated conditions, which we shall name the "ambiguity condition" (referred to as A), the "rumor condition" (referred to as R), and the "combined ambiguity-rumor condition" (A-R). In the two ambiguity conditions (A and A-R), the school principal interrupted work in several classes, pointed at one student, and announced: "Miss K, would you get your hat, coat, and books, please, and come with me. You will be gone for the rest of the day." Such an action was unprecedented in the experience of the students; it was intended to arouse a strong sense of ambiguity in their minds. In the two rumor conditions (R and again A-R), a rumor was planted with two girls in each of these classes. A day or two before the study, the girls were given appointments with their teacher to discuss academic progress and the next year's program. The appointments were routine, but during the interview the teacher asked "By the way, some examinations have been taken from the office. Do you happen to know anything about this?"

No theft had actually occurred. The rumor was simply intended to provide a ready explanation for why the principal had mysteriously summoned Miss K out of class. It was also timed so that the girls returned to their classrooms before the principal entered any of the rooms. In this way Schachter and Burdick could observe the amount of rumor that was subsequently spread in an ambiguous situation where a rumor was planted (condition A-R); when a rumor was planted with no accompanying ambiguity (condition R); and when ambiguity was present but no rumor planted (condition A).

The results of the experiments are given in Fig. 8, which shows the mean number of girls to whom the rumor was reportedly transmitted. We observe that there were twice as many exchanges of the rumor in the two ambiguity conditions (with or without the rumor!) than in the nonambiguity condition with the rumor. We also observe that the condition of a rumor *and* ambiguity resulted in the greatest average rate of transmission. Apparently, the ambiguity made a more substantial difference than the planted rumor. (When questioned later, nearly all the girls admitted they had heard the rumor at one time or another.) Thus the critical difference was in the dramatic nature of the staged incident between the principal and Miss K.

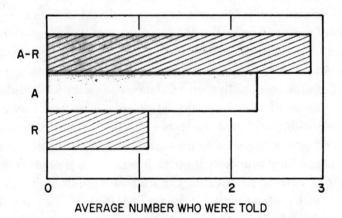

AVERAGE NUMBER WHO WERE TOLD

FIGURE 8. The average number of other students to whom the theft rumor was repeated in the experiment by Schachter and Burdick [221]. *(Adapted from data by permission of the first author)*

Schachter and Burdick also questioned the girls on the origin of new rumors, and these results are given in FIG. 9. We see that there was a large percentage of girls reporting new rumors in the two ambiguity conditions, but relatively few reporting new rumors in the nonambiguity condition. The staged incident provided a strong catalyst for the emergence of new tales as well as for the transmission of the deliberate rumor about missing exams. It appears that rumors arise when there is an exciting or mysterious event that has not been fully explained. That the greatest number of different rumors occurred in condition A-R implies a kind of "priming-the-pump" effect when a rumor is planted in a highly ambiguous situation: that is, rumor flow on one issue may promote a complementary flow on other issues.

The Anthony Experiment

This next experiment was carried out by social psychologist Susan Anthony, who experimented with anxiety as a possible causal factor [12]. Anthony made use of a small number of school children as subjects; boys and girls were randomly chosen from different clubs at a public high school. Several days before the study the students were administered a standard psychological measure of chronic anxiety developed by Taylor [245], known as the Manifest Anxiety Scale (MAS). On the basis of their scores on the MAS, two groups that were each either high or low in anxiety were selected for further observation. A few carefully selected members of these groups were scheduled to meet with their guidance counselor for an interview. During the course of the interview a false rumor was planted with the chosen students—because of budget limitations there would probably be a cut-back in extracurricular activities, and unfortunately their club was one activity that might be curbed. Afterwards, the student was left with fellow club members for a while, during which time all were free to talk with each other. At the end of this discussion period the group members rated the importance of cut-backs, were again administered the MAS, and were asked whether or not they had discussed the rumor.

The results are given in FIG. 10, and show that, indeed, there

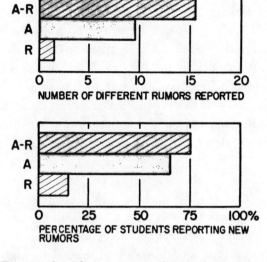

FIGURE 9. The variety and prevalence of new rumors in the experiment by Schachter and Burdick [221]. *(Adapted from data by permission of the first author)*

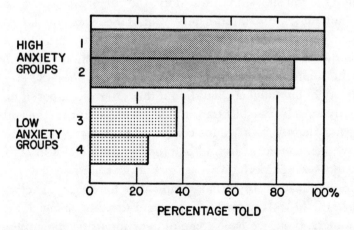

FIGURE 10. Percentage of members in two high and two low anxiety groups that were told the cut-back rumor in the experiment by Anthony [12]. *(Adapted from data by permission of the author)*

was substantially more rumormongering in the highly anxious groups than in those scoring lower on the MAS. Not shown in this figure are the before-after comparisons on anxiety or the students' ratings of importance. For these variables there were no appreciable differences: pre-test anxiety scores were roughly the same as the post-test scores, and there were no individual differences in the amount of rumor transmission that could be attributed to differences in the perceived importance of the issue.

Before turning to the next study, consider what we have learned so far. Schachter and Burdick presented evidence for the idea that rumor transmission varies with the ambiguity of the surrounding circumstances. They also inferred on the basis of some circumstantial evidence that their data might be supportive of the notion that there is more transmission of rumors under a state of "cognitive unclarity" when the issue is important than when it is unimportant. This, of course, we recognize as the full relationship hypothesized by Allport and Postman: $R = i \times a$. However, importance was not directly measured by Schachter and Burdick; their inference was not empirically substantiated, but based on routine uncontrolled observations. Indeed, Anthony found no differences in rated importance of a rumor between groups where there was little versus almost complete transmission of the story; the rumor was considered important by all. Unfortunately, importance was rated *after* the rumor was planted and allowed to circulate; we don't know whether the subject matter was equally important to all prior to the rumor manipulation. Anthony also examined the chronic anxiety of her subjects, and found that groups composed of highly anxious persons transmitted an important rumor with greater alacrity than groups composed of less anxious persons. However, she failed to find before-after differences in chronic anxiety—which perhaps weakens but does not necessarily refute the idea that rumormongering aims to reduce anxiety, since the MAS is notoriously resistant to acute changes. In summary, then, we have some direct support for the anbiguity variable, an apparent disagreement about the effects of importance as a variable, and equivocal evidence that anxiety is a basis of rumormongering.

The Biberian, Anthony, and Rosnow Experiment

This third experiment probed further into each of these elements [22]. Specifically, there are now three hypotheses to be tested. First, following Allport and Postman's assertion (and Schachter and Burdick's experimental findings) it can be predicted that the intensity of rumor flow is directly related to the ambiguity of the tale or situation. Second, also from Allport and Postman, it is expected that rumormongering is more apt to occur among those listeners who perceive the issue to be relatively important. Third, it is predicted that rumormongers (when contrasted with dead-enders) are shown as individuals who are characteristically high in anxiety.

To test the first hypothesis, a manipulation of ambiguity was sought, faithful to Allport and Postman's conception of rumormongering as an "effort after meaning" as well as to their definition of rumor [10, p. ix] as "a specific (or topical) proposition for belief, passed along from person to person, usually by word of mouth, without secure standards of evidence being present." From this definition it follows that once a standard of evidence has been established, there will be no more ambiguity and therefore the tale will no longer qualify as a rumor; it is then fact or fiction, depending on whether or not it was confirmed by the evidence at hand. One way to manipulate ambiguity is to pose a rumor in the form of a question ("Is it true that . . .?") and then to offer (or not offer) an acceptable standard of evidence [cf. 233].

In the present experiment this effect was achieved by planting a rumor in several college classes during the course of an orientation period. A confederate remarked to the class that he had heard a rumor about some students having smoked marijuana during a final exam the previous semester; he went on to ask whether anyone else had heard this rumor. In the *nonambiguity* condition, a second confederate quickly responded that the story was a complete hoax concocted by a friend of his, and that the friend was motivated to play a prank that would eventually reach the ear of the president of the university or the college newspaper. In the *ambiguity* condition, the second confederate instead responded that, yes, he had heard the rumor, but wasn't sure what to believe.

A few days before, the students had all been given a questionnaire containing the Manifest Anxiety Scale, other pertinent scales, and two questions on the importance of the issue of marijuana and other drug use. One week after the marijuana story was planted, the students were given another questionnaire asking whether they had spread the rumor; this questionnaire also contained some routine checks on how the conditions had been perceived and remembered.

The manipulation checks were consistent with expectations, and we can proceed to the tests of the three hypotheses. First, it was predicted that there would be more rumor flow in the ambiguity than in the nonambiguity condition. This result is given in FIG. 11, and we see that there was substantially more rumormongering reported in the ambiguity condition. Second, it was hypothesized that rumormongering was more likely to occur among those who perceived the issue of drug use to be of relative importance. There were two measures of importance in the pre-questionnaire. One measure concerned the use and control of drugs on a university campus; this item was rated significantly higher in importance by nontransmitters than by transmitters. The other measure concerned the legalization of marijuana, and on this item there was no appreciable difference in rated importance by transmitters versus nontransmitters. Hence, the only significant effect was exactly opposite to what had been hypothesized on the basis of Allport and Postman's formula. Third, it was also predicted that rumormongers would be characterized by a significantly higher degree of chronic anxiety than nontransmitters, and these results were as expected.

Thus we have further evidence of the effects of ambiguity and anxiety as consistent with the findings by Schachter and Burdick and by Anthony (who used different research populations and subjected them to entirely different manipulations). Contrary to Allport and Postman, the perceived importance of the issue did not operate in the way predicted by their for-

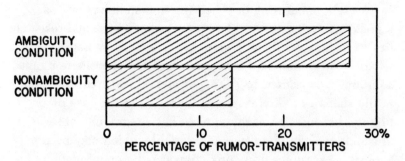

FIGURE 11. Percentage of students in the ambiguity and nonambiguity conditions that reported they had passed the marijuana rumor in the experiment by Biberian, Anthony, and Rosnow.

mula. The importance finding was not at variance with Anthony's observations, however, and one may conclude that the actual *level* of importance (beyond some minimal degree) may not be a critical variable in rumor flow. It is plausible that in some instances an issue may not be perceived as being very important until after the fact, the perception of importance being an elaborate rationalization for having expended time and energy in talking or thinking about the subject. In fig. 11 we also see that even in the nonambiguity condition there was evidence of rumor flow. We know that denial is not absolutely foolproof for quashing a rumor, and in some cases (the McCartney rumor, for example) there can be a boomerang effect when one sets out to repudiate a rumor. It is plausible that the very act of denial raises doubts and thereby provides a further basis for ambiguity and innuendo.

However, the findings in these three experiments also imply that there must be other factors besides ambiguity and anxiety at work, or these few simple relationships would have been more definitive.

OTHER STUDIES

Experimental research, in which variables are manipulated to elicit possible causal relationships, is one means of scientific inquiry. One can also discover important co-relationships by carefully measuring or observing human behavior in a non-experimental setting. The power of experimental research lies in the answer it can give to the question: "What leads to what?" Where non-experimental research yields the tentative solution "X *is related to* Y," experimental research can result in the statement "X is *responsible* for Y." In the case of ambiguity, because it was manipulated as a temporal antecedent of rumor, we can identify it as a variable which may be responsible for rumor flow. Anxiety was not a manipulated variable, so we only know that it is related to increased rumor flow; we do not know if it is actually responsible for that increase. We do know, however, that anxiety reduction is an explicit or implicit assumption of the various theories and other observations surveyed in chapters 3 and 4, whereas ambiguity is emphasized by many, but not all, researchers or theorists. Before considering other, non-experimental studies, let us try to guess how these two variables co-operate based on the limited information we possess.

Earlier we used the analogy of the synapse to characterize the dissemination of rumor. We now hypothesize that chronic anxiety is like a transmitter chemical which aids in the transfer of the excitation from one neuron to another. When anxieties are concentrated, they increase the efficiency of rumor transmission (although there is a point at which too much anxiety weakens transmission). Ambiguity is the energy used to excite the neuron. Just as in nature this energy is nonspecific, rumor flow occurs in response to other excitations besides ambiguity. We observed that there was some rumormongering even when there was presumably little or no ambiguity; and in the experiment by Schachter and Burdick there was a preponderance of new rumors caused by the "excitement" of ambiguity. Thus there are numerous sources of intense energy to excite the potential rumormonger and to shape the construction and dissemination of different types of rumors. Indeed, we find hints of such variables in some non-experimental studies—but before turning to those clues, let us examine more closely the idea of anxiety as a transmitter chemical and ambiguity as the energy that fuels the potential rumormonger.

The Smock Experiment

The missing link in this chain of logical inference is sup-
plied in a study by Smock. Prior to this experiment it had been
shown that many people have a relatively low tolerance for
ambiguity, and that some (those who are highly ethnocentric
or authoritarian) are more intolerant of ambiguity [4, 81, 82].
Smock tested the hypothesis that psychological stress will also
tend to increase this intolerance for ambiguity [234].

He presented a series of cards to a large sample of research
subjects. Each card depicted a different drawing—a naked
woman standing in a bathtub, a man digging with a shovel, the
number "5", a bird, a kitten, an ornamental vase. There were
pictures of each that varied in their degree of clarity. Some
pictures were so highly ambiguous as to be unidentifiable;
some were perfectly clear; the others were on a scale ranging
between these two extremes. The instructions to the research
subjects were to organize the ambiguous elements into the
complete design or picture with as few cards as possible. Some
of the research subjects (chosen at random) had to do this
under stressful conditions: the experimenter treating them as if
they had failed to measure up to normal expectations. The
other subjects performed the task under nonstressful conditions: the experimenter assuring them that the task itself was
being studied and not their individual performance. The results supported Smock's hypothesis. The subjects who worked
under psychological stress responded much more quickly (and
prematurely) to the cards, which suggests that the stressful
situation had increased their intolerance for ambiguity.

People are easily made anxious by stress circumstances.
Given that external stress can be equated with internal anxiety, and from what we know about the relationship between
anxiety, ambiguity, and rumor flow, it is now a short step to
the tentative conclusion that anxiety is an incipient mood
highly conducive to rumormongering because it increases the
intolerance for ambiguity.

Non-experimental Findings

We consider now some other variables which might plausibly serve as triggering conditions for rumor. In an unpublished survey conducted early in 1970, the first author, with the assistance of George Gitter, Susan Anthony, and Robert M. Gordon, interviewed a large number of college students in an effort to delineate some of the characteristics of those who spread or didn't spread the Paul McCartney rumor [cf. 214]. It was felt at the time that rumormongers must be different from others, and we hoped to discover sharp individual differences between these two types. We found instead that the dissemination of the Paul McCartney rumor was bound more to the situation than to a cluster of individual difference variables. There were virtually no appreciable differences between rumormongers and dead-enders on a host of demographic and biographical variables. However, one promising clue did emerge: on the assumption that rumor flow requires a fertile breeding ground, the rumormongers were expected to be sociable and have many friends with whom to share the rumor. Surprisingly, they were less popular; they dated less often and got together with friends less frequently than did nonrumormongers. This interesting finding appeared to confirm something else reported by Schachter and Burdick in their experiment. They had also anticipated that good friends would circulate new rumors more than would mere acquaintances. However, 68 percent of friends reported discussing stories other than the planted rumor about the missing exam, but 74 percent of acquaintances reported this. Many of the rumors were distinctly unfavorable to the missing girl ("She's being disciplined for going to a wild party last weekend."), and these were more prevalent in discussions among acquaintances than among friends also [221]. The results lead us to guess that rumormongering may sometimes be an attempt to gain esteem. Someone without many friends might worry about his or her self-esteem, and he or she might pass on a titillating rumor in hope of building a new friendship. The recipient of the rumor bestows status on the rumormonger merely by accepting it. Indeed, in the case of the Paul McCartney rumor one could argue that the story died because there arose a point of diminishing returns for the status-seeker. Eventually, nothing new could be added to the tale, and any teller gained minimally and may even have lost status by continuing to be obsessed by the mystery.

The effort after status, like the effort after meaning, is a plausible triggering condition in both the construction and dissemination of rumor. The common focus is an instrumentalist perspective, which argues that rumor is "caused" by certain human needs. Where the need is for information or clarity, rumor fills the void of ambiguity and uncertainty. Where other needs or hopes predominate, they in turn mold the form of rumors that are need-fulfilling. Thus rumors arise when there is any exciting or mysterious event that has not been fully explained. They also appear when someone (the enemy agent in time of war or the "dirty trickster" in a political campaign) seeks to gain a competitive advantage by planting malicious tales or false strategic information. We are told that in a mayoralty election in New York City in the 1960s, a few active supporters of one major nominee deliberately dropped rumors about rival candidates during "private" discussions on the subway, in elevators, and in other public places. The talk was just loud enough to be "overheard" by others nearby, who (it was assumed) would then pass on the story in the normal course of conversation. Information that does not seem directly intended for our ears may be all the more persuasive because it catches us when our defenses are down; like any commodity, it is also precious because it is privileged and scarce [cf. 32, 84, 264]. Information is also instrumentally valuable if it seems to provide the recipient with social evidence of the validity of his opinions and behavior, to let him know that he is keeping pace with the herd [cf. 50, 63].

Another correlational study, by Floyd H. Allport and Milton Lepkin [5], is suggestive of possible triggering conditions. Although a rumor may appeal to universal needs (as Jung argued) not every individual in society necessarily hears the rumor, and not everyone who has heard it believes it. This variability could be a function of individual differences, and the study by Allport and Lepkin was essentially the prototype of investigations on this subject.

The Allport and Lepkin study was conducted during World War II. A questionnaire was constructed containing a dozen rumors about waste and special privilege, and was then distributed to parents of several hundred grade and high school students in Syracuse, New York. The following are examples of the rumors used:

The canning companies are holding large stocks of canned goods for higher prices.

Scrap rubber collected is wasted by being allowed to deteriorate because there are no adequate facilities for storage and reclaiming.

A certain government official has three cars and a large underground storage tank filled with gasoline for his own use.

Among the elements found to lend credence to rumors such as these was the fondness for a good story and the desire to be the center of attention. These factors can easily fit into a social exchange framework; they represent both sides of an information/esteem transaction, in the manner of transactions in the Paul McCartney rumor. In return for a good story, the teller receives the listener's esteem. How well this reciprocal exchange of resources functions determines the longevity of the rumor.

It was also observed that hearing a familiar rumor made it appear more credible. Recently other psychologists have noted this phemonenon whereby repeated exposure to a message can make it more readily acceptable [267]. Like some grating, repetitious commercials, on repeated exposure they do not seem so difficult to accept after all. The effect can be explained by assuming that the learning which accompanies re-exposure is satisfying because it increases our understanding of environmental complexities by simplifying them. This positive emotion then becomes attached to the message. Once the message is well learned, boredom sets in and causes it to appear in a less favorable light, creating an optimum level of exposure [232, 236].

Another finding by Allport and Lepkin was that belief in the credibility of these rumors was greater among individuals who doubted that other people were giving their all to the war effort, and it was also greater among those who experienced personal inconveniences. People's frustrations made them more apt to attribute selfish motives to others, pointing out the ego-defensive function of rumor as emphasized by Festinger and Jung. Another finding suggested a possible "immunizing" effect of repeated exposure to a newspaper column which analyzed and refuted rumors. However, as noted earlier, this result was not clear-cut; the differences in beliefs might have been due to a more critical readership being drawn to the newspaper column in the first place. Other findings of individual differences were that men believed these malicious rumors more than women, and that middle-aged people believed them more than younger adults.

Thus we find that the frustrations and inconveniences which people encountered as a result of rationing programs may have been displaced in a way that made wedge-driving rumors easier to believe. Acceptance of these rumors was especially high among those who were skeptical that others were doing their fair share. Indeed, any strong need or wish might be the energy that fuels the rumor and starts it on its way.

THE SOCIAL EXCHANGE PARADIGM

The transactional nature of human interaction, in particular the parallel with economic theory [130], is a familiar theme in modern sociology [24, 46, 114, 115, 156], social anthropology [17, 185, 186], and social psychology [1, 79, 88, 246]; and this view is ideally suited to rumormongering. From the broader perspective of social exchange, one can readily visualize rumormongering as a transaction in which someone passes a rumor for something in return—another rumor, clarifying information, status, power, control, money, or some other resource. When information is scarce, the rumormonger can exact a high price for his tales. When the market for rumors expands, the number of rumors will proliferate. If the exchange is mutually rewarding, it should result in some structural relationship in which future exchanges can be more easily transacted. The person who repeatedly gives good information when other sources are unavailable or unreliable is providing a scarce, highly valued commodity. These transactions, when the producer is rewarded with attention, admiration, money, or any valued resource, result in a stratification within the group with the producer acquiring more status than the other members [115]. However, "prosperity" can also dig its own grave: a society deprived of hard news and therefore prospering on rumors becomes skeptical, suspicious, and increasingly close-mouthed.

The parallel between rumormongering and marketplace psychology breaks down when considering the motivational basis of the transaction. In contrast to classical economic theory, which postulates a single, comprehensive motive, it appears that in rumormongering multiple motives are at work. On a conscious or unconscious level, rumormongering strives to gratify individual and group needs. The need to understand the environment is a prime motive that appeared on different levels of analysis, although a wide variety of other motives was also suggested. Unfortunately, we cannot yet specify the circumstances in which certain motives are prevalent.

Also in contrast to classical economic theory is the phenomenological view of valuation in social exchange. Firstly, it would be an obvious mistake to assume that, in all cases, man's economic behavior is rational—always maximizing his options and arriving at that which makes the most sense in short and long term rewards and costs. People do not act on objective rational choice, but on whatever seems to be appropriate under the circumstances. This phenomenological view explains why there is so much individual variation in rumormongering. Each person attaches different weights to his options, and behavior can differ widely in similar circumstances. Secondly, man is not always deliberate in determining his course of action; he usually acts on sketchy information and does not often weigh various alternatives. Thirdly, his behavior will be a function (in part) of his perceptions of the demands and etiquette of the situation.

The question arises of how people know what they know. Belief in a certain rumor can alter one's perceptions of the world and create a new semblance of reality. The classical sociological dictum states that if situations are defined as real, they will be real in their consequences. Robert Merton has extended this notion with the idea of the self-fulfilling prophecy [169]—rumors about shortages, bank runs, and stock prices are examples stressing the complicated social nature of these situational definitions [169, 209, 223]. However, most prophecies are not self-fulfilling, and it is thought that rumors must be closely understood within a given social context in order to sustain action. Economic psychologist George Katona writes [130, p. 660]:

> Mass behavior consisting of cumulative and self-justifying expectations may be viewed as a form of catastrophic behavior. The masses resist speculative fever or despondency unless their sanity is crushed by a series of repeated shocks. The basis of mass sanity may be found in the desire to understand the reasons for developments that take place. News and rumors which are not clearly understood may be accepted for a short while, but will not sustain action by very many people over long periods.

While the rational model of the rumormonger as an objective information processor would be far too simple a conceptualization, this does not mean that an exchange framework cannot be an illuminating paradigm for grasping the workings of social

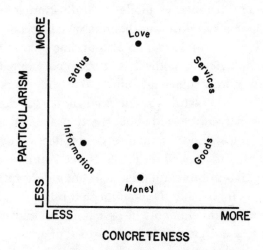

FIGURE 12. Resource theory, postulated by Uriel and Edna Foa, assumes that there is a structural pattern in the interrelationship of the six general resources as shown above. *(After Foa [78] by permission of the author and* Science *magazine)*

exchange. Uriel and Edna Foa have recently demonstrated how there may be a stuctural pattern in the interrelationships among six general classes of social resources: information, status, love, services, goods, and money [78, 79]. They have plotted these on a two-coordinate space (see FIG. 12) according to their "particularism" (the significance of the person providing the resource) and "concreteness" (whether the resource is symbolic or conceptually concrete). Information falls between status and money in this diagram. It was found that adjoining resources are perceived as similar and that people usually reciprocate or retaliate in kind when they are given or have had to give up some specified resource. The Foas did not mean this formulation to be directly applicable to rumor exchange (except possibly where the rumor is purely informative and therefore fits neatly into the information category), but it is a promising start towards a precise theory of social exchange.

In summary, then, we have postulated a theoretical abstraction for further empirical inquiry. We have, as Heisenberg observed with reference to all abstractions in modern science [106], merely "a basic structure, a sort of skeleton, which only the addition of a great wealth of further details could turn into a genuine picture."

The value of this tentative model is in illustrating certain common properties of different theories which can be integrated by a hybrid paradigm, and also in dramatizing that the familiar psychological hypothesis stating rumormongering is a joint function of importance and ambiguity is an oversimplification. Unfortunately, at this stage in our understanding there is little more that can be said about the transactional nature of rumormongering without prematurely complicating the theoretical structure. Social exchange is not a simple and sovereign motive in human interaction, but a descriptive framework for simplifying the complicated rules of behavior. It reduces the thematic elements in psychological and sociological theories to a unifying paradigm, instead of arguing that any one hypothesis or motive in rumormongering is exclusively valid or invalid. Let us now turn to a closer analysis of the nature of gossip, also well suited for this skeletal abstraction.

six : : *Gossip:Rumor Writ Small*

There are two kinds of people who blow through life like a breeze, And one kind is gossipers, and the other kind is gossipees.

OGDEN NASH
I'm a Stranger Here Myself

The poet's assertion notwithstanding, each of us at one time or another has been both gossiper and gossipee. The degree and nature of our involvement in gossiping will vary, as gossiping is a transitory behavior. It is possible that a persistent tendency to gossip is in part a character trait or personality disposition, although there is no psychological evidence in support of this hypothesis. In fact, little is known about the psychology of gossiping, why some people seldom gossip and others gossip a great deal, or about the psychological differences between Ogden Nash's "gossipers" and "gossipees".

We are all familiar with the common stereotype that brands gossiping as a feminine pastime (see FIG. 13). Leo Rosten, the writer, mentions that the Yiddish word for a gossipy woman, *yenta,* is a sexist slur especially when used to describe a man [216]. However, this old stereotype may be just an artifact de-

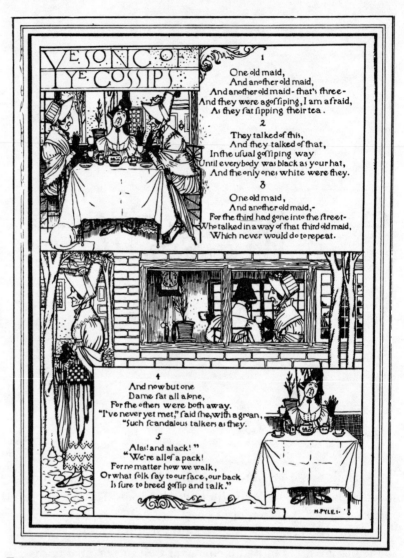

One old maid,
And another old maid,
And another old maid - that's three -
And they were agossiping, I am afraid,
As they sat sipping their tea.

2

They talked of this,
And they talked of that,
In the usual gossiping way
Until everybody was black as your hat,
And the only ones white were they.

3

One old maid,
And another old maid, -
For the third had gone into the street -
Who talked in a way of that third old maid,
Which never would do to repeat.

4

And now but one
Dame sat all alone,
For the others were both away.
"I've never yet met," said she, with a groan,
"Such scandalous talkers as they.

5

Alas! and alack!"
"We're all of a pack!
For no matter how we walk,
Or what folk say to our face, our back
Is sure to breed gossip and talk."

H. PYLE.

FIGURE 13. The stereotype of the gossipy woman is captured by the American writer and illustrator Howard Pyle in his line-drawing entitled "Ye Song of Ye Gossips." The drawing was originally published in 1885. *(Collection of Howard Pyle Brokaw, photograph courtesy of Brandywine River Museum)*

riving from the semantics of the situation. What is usually called gossip or "gabbing" among women is called "shop talk" or "shooting the breeze" when it is done by men. Because the connotations are vastly different, this perhaps has tended to obscure the denotative similarity. The term "gabfest", for example, was coined to describe a particularly prolonged and empty debate among congress*men*. How "gabbing" came to refer to female loquaciousness is a mystery [167]. One need not search very far to find gossipy men. Magazines for men and women, trade books, and novels all contain a wide range of gossip by and about both sexes. Indeed, at this writing, the non-fiction best-seller in the United States is the gossipy revelation of the First Family's behavior during the Watergate incident which led to Richard M. Nixon's resignation from the Presidency—the book by Bob Woodward and Carl Bernstein *The Final Days.*

While not much has been empirically established about gossiping as a personality or as a "biological" disposition, there have been some wildly fanciful speculations. At the turn of the century it was claimed that there might be "an essential identity between the gossip and the genius." The argument went that both types have great intellectual curiosity, excellent recall, and the ability to make novel and original connections between events. The genius can distinguish between relevant and irrelevant ideas, where the gossiper presumably cannot. The "sin of gossiping" was said to be due to a person's neural organization, and the conclusion [155, p. 106] was drawn that "they [gossipers] are rather to be pitied than condemned, because their garrulity and scandalizing are the nature and inevitable outcome of peculiar brain processes."

THE NATURE OF GOSSIP

Just as there is uncertainty about the profile of the gossiper, there is ambiguity in the operational meaning of gossip. The unabridged *Random House Dictionary* gives rumor as a synonym for gossip, which it defines as "idle talk". Niehoff, however, has suggested drawing a distinction between "positive gossip" and "negative gossip," and preserving rumor as a synonym for the latter expression [180]. Cooley writes that rumor deals with events and gossip deals with people [49], but Thomas and Znaniecki have qualified this distinction slightly in arguing that rumor deals only with important events and gossip deals with trivial personal occurrences [249]. Blumenthal sees in gossip the unorganized dispersal of information [26, p. 36]: "All unregimented dissemination of information would be considered gossiping regardless of whether the information was scientifically accurate or erroneous. However, it is important to note that regimentation exists relative to the regimentor."

Whether or not experts have been able to concur on a definition of gossip, it is not very difficult to intuitively decide whether something is or isn't gossip. Gossip is small talk, or tattling about someone—a preoccupation with the "nonessential"—and the news may or may not be factual. Lumley [158, p. 215] calls it "intellectual chewing gum." There is, to be sure, a bias towards ascribing one's own "small talk" to legitimate information trading and the small talk of others to gossiping or scandalmongering. This is quite natural, considering the usual reputation of gossipers. However, most of us seem able to agree on what constitutes gossip in everyday conversation. The elements of familiarity and informality are relevant cues to the consideration of how conversation is popularly classified.

Part of the difficulty social scientists have in arriving at a convergent definition of gossip, is defined by the context in which it appears. As Hannerz remarks [102]: "The same information may be gossip or non-gossip depending on who gives it to whom; the communication that Mrs. A's child is illegitimate is not gossip if it is occurring between two social workers acting in that capacity, while it is gossip if Mrs. A's neighbors talk about it." In the first instance the communication contains news that is relevant and significant to the disposition of her case; it is not merely "idle talk." In the second instance, it is tattling; the conversation is "illegitimate" as well as the child. Through knowledge of the source's intentions and legitimate rights to or interest in the information, we determine if it is, or is not, gossip. Hannerz also makes the point that gossiping is a kind of meta-communication—in other words, communication about communication.

By this broad definition, there must be a point at which rumor and gossip semantically intertwine. This occurs when news is unsubstantiated and focuses on some interesting but objectively trivial, personal highlight. At this point the two concepts are equivalent. The result is androgynous hearsay, as illustrated by the McCartney tale. However, except for this aberrant derivative, gossip is distinguished from rumor by the fact that its life cycle usually evolves more rapidly, and therefore is not as easily divisible into distinct stages. Indeed those examples of gossip which appear to have recognizable life histories are most closely akin to rumor. For this reason, the "life cycle" is not an especially good metaphor for describing the stages of gossip. With gossip there appears to be a rapid metamorphosis rather than a step-like ascent and descent. The usual piece of gossip does not die, but instead evaporates. Gossip begins as an amorphous, stationary mass when the psychological atmosphere is very cool; it quickly becomes a dripping, dribbling, then flowing substance that seaps and envelops as the temperature heats up; and it finally vaporizes in thin air.

One characteristic of gossip which is shared with rumor is its derogatory connotation. In her final work entitled *Daniel Deronda,* the Victorian novelist George Eliot observed: "Gossip is a sort of smoke that comes from the dirty tobacco-pipes of those who diffuse it; it proves nothing but the bad taste of the smoker." Gossip and scandal are seen to go hand in hand [92]. Note also the following graphic account as expressed by LeGallienne after the turn of the century [151]:

According to the old Scandinavian fable of the cosmos, the whole world is encircled in the coils of a vast serpent . . . Still, as of old, the world is encircled . . . and the name of the serpent is Gossip. Wherever man is, there may you hear its sibilant whisper, and its foul spawn squirm and sting and poison in nests of hidden noisomeness myriad as the spores of corruption in a putrefying carcass, varying in size from some hydra-headed infamy endangering whole nations and even race with its deadly breath, to the microscopic wrigglers that multiply, a million a minute, in the covered cesspools of private life.

Printed history is so infested with this vermin, in the form of secret memoirs, back-stairs diarists, and boudoir eavesdroppers, that it is almost impossible to feel sure of the actual fact of any history whatsoever. The fame of great personages may be literally compared to the heroic figures in the well-known group of the Laocoon, battling in vain with the strangling coils of the sea-serpent of Poseidon. We scarcely know what to believe of the dead; and for the living, is it not true, as Tennyson puts it, that "each man walks with his head in a cloud of poisonous flies?"

In tracing the various usages of the term, one finds many instances in which gossip is regarded scornfully. Hesiod, around 700 B.C., wrote that it was "mischievous . . . grievous to bear." The *Talmud* admonished Jewish men not to gossip with women, not even with their own wives, the assumption apparently being that this "idle chatter" has a way of becoming purposeful and turning to the forbidden topic of sex (Maimonides, circa 1200). The British writer H. H. Munro (Saki) said of gossip: "Hating anything in the way of ill-natured gossip ourselves, we are always grateful to those who do it for us and do it well" (*Reginald in Russia*, 1910). Poet Robert Burns immortalized the mischievous allure of a juicy bit of gossip:

> Oh ye wha are sae gude yoneaivl,
> Sae pious and sae holy;
> Ye've naught to do but mark and tell
> Your neighbor's faults and folly.

However, gossip has not always, or universally, been treated with scorn. The term is derived from the Old English *godsibb*, for God-parent. It came to mean any friend or acquaintance of the parents of the baptized child or of the other God-parents. It was also at one time an expression for the women friends of the child's mother who were present at the birth and "idly chattered" among themselves. Obviously there is nothing sinister or scornful in any of these usages. Even as recently as the late nineteenth century, we find instances in which gossiping was favorably regarded. Ralph Waldo Emerson once wrote: "Our globe discovers its hidden virtues not only in heroes, and archangels, but in gossips and nurses" (*Representative Men*, 1860). In another example, from Lumley, we find [158, pp. 212–213]:

> In 1888 the girls of North Hall, Newnham, debated the question whether life without gossip would be worth living. The vote was unanimously negative, and Miss Gladstone, the principal, defended this most just decision. However, she understood gossip to mean ready, informed and piquent conversation . . . "Foul whispering," a vulgar and shamelessly undressed tattling was furthest from her thought.

Niehoff's [180] distinction between "positive" and "negative" gossip is not really essential to its definition, and we shall therefore broadly define gossip as nonessential (often trivial) news about someone. Gossip can thus refer to news about the affairs of another, to one's own memoirs or confessions, or to any hearsay of a personal nature, be it positive or negative, spoken or in print. In that shadowy area between gossip and rumor, where the significance of the message is unclear or debatable, either term will suffice. The question now posed is how something characterized as "trivial" can be of value as a social resource: the answer once again lies in the myriad functions of gossip.

GOSSIP AS SOCIAL EXCHANGE

Ideas about the functions of gossip are as varied as those of the functions of rumor [237]. Unfortunately, psychologists have not paid as much attention to gossip as to rumor, nor have they studied gossip to the extent that anthropologists and sociologists have. While this results in there being little to say, empirically, about individual difference variables—usually considered the domain of psychology—the literature is rich with ideas about how gossip is used in individual impression management, how it exerts control over the behavior of others, and how it functions in general for the community at large. As with rumor, social exchange provides the underlying theme in gossiping: a transaction is made in which news is exchanged for some desired resource. Like rumormongering, gossiping appears to be mediated by subtle anxieties and thus seems directed at reducing or avoiding possible strains or diffusing a discomfort. This is not to say that gossiping cannot arouse anxiety; but one person's dissatisfaction may be a source of comfort to another.

The transactional nature of small talk is most vividly illustrated by the gossip columnist, a tradition which in this country goes back to 1730, when Benjamin Franklin wrote a column for the *Pennsylvania Gazette* [247]. Mark Twain wrote a column for the Virginia City *Enterprise* and the Sacramento

Union. Eugene Field contributed to the Chicago *News* ("Sharps and Flats") and Bert Leston Taylor, to the Chicago *Tribune* ("A line o' Type or Two"). In New York, Franklin P. Adams began his column in the *Mail* in 1911, and the Broadway column was first popularized by S. Jay Kaufman, writing in the *Mail* and *Globe.* Walter Winchell advanced the art to its penultimate degree by his syndicated column in the Hearst newspapers and his radio program whose trademark was the familiar greeting: "Good evening, Mr. and Mrs. America and all the ships at sea. Let's go to press. . . ."

Americans are notoriously consumption-oriented [204, 205], and the conspicuous consumption of gossip attests to the wide generality of this habit. However, there are class preferences in the consumption of gossip that affect the behavior, supply, and inventories of its producers and distributors. In some cases a high degree of cost consciousness is required, for if what one must pay—in psychological terms—becomes too high, the quantity demanded will probably decline. In other cases, finding a "bargain" is of little concern, and there may even be an element of snobbery in paying a little more for gossip as a commodity.

Consumers of gossip have their own brand loyalties; they are faithful to certain columnists, tabloids, and magazines. Indeed, because of the vast market for gossip, there are employment opportunities in both the print and electronic media for specialists on backstairs happenings. The symbiotic relationship between producer and consumer is a casebook example. For the producer, the reward is money, recognition, and the power to be able to "manage the news." For the consumer, the gratification is in the entertainment provided, the diversion from the tedium of everyday life, the feeling of being a privileged insider, and the perverse delight in knowing the shortcomings and misfortunes of successful people. The reviewer of a book of Hollywood gossip, which contained such venomous barbs as the story of a prominent movie director who was killed along with his 14-year old paramour while attempting simultaneously to drive an automobile and indulge in a homosexual act, described his own reaction as being like the morbid fascination of witnessing the aftermath of a terrible accident.

While the telling and reading of gossip may be morbidly or perversely satisfying, the gratification which results from the dynamics of the relationship between the teller and the reader is decidedly unbalanced. Let the buyer beware, for the power dynamics are tilted in favor of the producer and not the consumer. Gossip columnists have an uncanny ability to persuade the masses. Walter Winchell was a staunch supporter of President Franklin D. Roosevelt, and actively propagandized on behalf of the New Deal. Drew Pearson's "Washington Merry Go-Round" is political exposé after exposé, a column now in its second generation. Through the use of planted gossip, Hollywood columnists like Hedda Hopper and Louella Parsons helped to create an aura of "stardom" around numerous motion picture personalities.

The pattern of the diffusion of this information corresponds to a two-step flow process [132, 149]. News flows from political leaks, insiders, press departments, and the personalities themselves to the gossip columnist, and from there to the rank-and-file [260]. The reporter acts as a gate-keeper who channels the flow of information. One intriguing side effect of all this is that the gate-keeper as well becomes a fitting subject of gossip. Louella Parsons once commented [67, p. 177]: "I have been sniped at by experts. And why not? Almost everyone who has attained any kind of public stature in his or her profession can expect sometimes to see a reflection in a cracked mirror."

Economic anthropologists speak of three patterns of economic exchange [190]. First, a reciprocative system is illustrated by the ritualized give-and-take of gossip at cocktail parties; gossip is exchanged because it is traditional to do so, and the only guiding principle is that the exchange should "balance out" in the long run. A second pattern is termed simply, exchange; commodities are brought into the marketplace and bargaining is done for economic advantage. Thus, after President Nixon resigned, one of his former advisors, H. R. Haldeman, agreed to divulge certain Watergate information in return for a fat fee from the Columbia Broadcasting System. More recently, Nixon himself has agreed to a highly remunerative arrangement by which he will supposedly reveal inside information in a series of interviews for television consumption. A third pattern, termed redistributive, is an apt description of the entrepreneurial two-step flow of information: news is brought to a central source, the gossip columnist, and then redistributed throughout the populace.

Gossip has also been considered as a means of preserving status. The more exclusive or highly organized the group, the more gossip there is within it. Social anthropologist Max Gluckman lists three types of groups that employ gossip in this way [92]. One is the professional group (lawyers, educators, physicians) in which gossip is interwoven with technical terms and is practically indecipherable to the outsider. Gluckman writes [92, p. 309]:

> This is, therefore, the most irritating kind of group to crash into, because one has no clue to the undercurrents, no apparatus for taking soundings. And this is why old practitioners of a subject can so easily put a comparative newcomer into his place, can make him feel a neophyte. They have only to hint in a technical argument at some personal fact about the person who advanced the theory discussed, to make the eager young student feel how callow he is.

A second type is social groups that seek to preserve their exclusiveness by closing the doors to parvenus. Because membership is often inherited, one must have distinguished ancestors or celebrated friends. To be a true insider, one must know and be able to gossip about the present membership as well as their forebears. By the same token, the gossiper himself must be worthy of discussion, or else he or she will be considered the parvenu.

The third type of group is that which has exclusiveness thrust upon it—for example, an ethnic or minority group. Elizabeth Colson's study of the Makah Indians, who live in the Puget Sound area opposite Vancouver Island, illustrates how gossiping is adaptive in that it keeps individuals in their assigned places in the social order [47]. In the *potlach* system a member of the tribe is obligated to give feasts to demonstrate his high hereditary status. However, because in theory anyone can now earn enough money to give a feast, the *potlach* is no longer a reliable means of ascribing status. Gossip serves this purpose instead, and in so doing helps to preserve the unity of a tribe which finds security from the inequality of a structured class system.

There have been numerous such accounts by anthropologists of this manipulative use of gossiping within a community. When there is a political threat from without, gossip can be a very potent propaganda weapon for uniting the group from within. Cox studied the use of gossip during a political power struggle among progressive and traditionalist factions on a Hopi Indian reservation in Northeastern Arizona [51]. One side spread the word that the other side was a "bunch of Communists" who wanted to practice human sacrifice. The other side countered that its opponents were materialistic toadies who were selling out to the White Establishment.

Cox cites gossiping as an example of what sociologists call a "degradation ceremony" [cf. 85]. Within every community there is an etiquette for gossiping, and one who doesn't follow the rules is seen and treated as a deviant. In the medical community there is gossip that is considered proper and gossip that is considered improper; proper gossip is that indulged in by all M.D.s, which preserves the status of the profession; improper gossip aims at raising the teller's self-esteem at the expense of his professional peers [52]. Thus again we observe that gossip is not merely *idle* talk, but talk with a social purpose. Like gamesmanship, the art of winning games without actually cheating, the etiquette of what is proper and improper in gossiping is rigidly controlled [92].

Treading the thin line between impressions and reality, this kind of gossiping can be a potent force for wreaking vengence. Talk about someone's drinking or sexual habits can strip away his respectability. In a more subtle example, there is the case of the psychoanalyst who used an important patient's free associations for stock market tips. The analysis ended unsuccessfully. However, the patient, who discovered his doctor's unscrupulous breach of confidence, had the considerable satisfaction of then passing along a particularly poor tip [52].

This vengeful gossip, when directed at an in-group member, can be quite disruptive of group harmony, and in many preliterate societies there are formalized and supernatural sanctions for controlling it. Stirling reports that among the West African Ashanti, tale-bearing is considered a serious breach of etiquette that must be publicly punished. If the target is someone of high status within the tribe, the perpetrator either has his lips cut off or is executed. However, the Ashanti also recognize the need for catharsis and therefore hold ceremonies for venting the pent-up emotions engendered by interpersonal hostilities. Stirling notes that among the Seminole Indians of the American Southeast "talking bad about anyone" is regarded in the same category as lying and stealing; participation in such activities can lessen the chances of ever reaching "Big Ghost City" in one's spirit life after death [237].

Gossip also offers a means of passing time and, as chit-chat, helps to maintain the fluidity of communication patterns. Even in a small community there are information specialists and news carriers [241]. Like the psychoanalyst who was too busy to seek information himself, but was quick to make use of his patient's efforts, gossip collectors can be employed by those preoccupied or too discreet to gather information themselves. Parents routinely use children as news runners. Children have the ability to obtain information and to engage in encounters which might jeopardize an adult's reputation. The exchange function is nicely illustrated by the old cartoon showing the younger sibling extracting a bribe from his sister and her beau in exchange for not telling his parents what he has seen.

Gossip is also the repository of folklore and taboo and in some cultures it is a storehouse for legal precedents. Memorable judicial cases of past generations are encoded in the gossip of the Zuni Indians of the American Southwest [206]. In the Tztotzil-speaking community of Chiapas, on the Yucatan Peninsula of Mexico, gossip reaffirms cultural norms and values by stressing moral sanctions [105]. An extreme case illustrating this function is that of a young woman who took her own life, driven to it by the vicious talk of several old crones in the quiet English village where they all lived [158]. Their gossip ruined her good name, and when faced with flight or death, she tragically chose to commit suicide. The coroner's jury, after examining the circumstances of her death, brought in the verdict "killed by idle gossip."

In this case it might be said that the gossip served an ego need on the part of the gossipers—the need to reaffirm values and social etiquette. The case might also be interpreted as an expression of sentiments and attitudes, or as a confirmation of prejudices [cf. 131]. Malicious gossip, if it serves a deep-seated need on the part of the gossiper, requires a delicate balance between his wishes and actions. In his memoir, *Inside the Third Reich,* Albert Speer tells of German scientists who could have developed an atomic bomb as early as 1945, had it not been for Hitler's prejudice against what he referred to as "Jewish physics." If actions are too strong, they can destroy the object and deprive the gossiper of further gratification. Some political gossip in the press also serves as an example: there is an unconscious wish to preserve the negative object in order to fulfill the journalist's need for good copy, but if the object is not attacked or exposed it can lose the attributes that have made it provocative and worthy of editorial comment.

An interesting and little studied form of gossiping is the autobiography, in particular that of the "confessional" variety. Theodor Reik, the Freudian psychoanalyst, described a basic personality type, the masochist, who degrades and humiliates himself in the pursuit of love [203]. If the masochist is ingratiating or gossips abusively about himself, it is to achieve this one goal of being loved. Personality psychologist Sidney Jourard observed that certain individuals have an unusually strong tendency for self-disclosure [125]—again possibly a form of ingratiation.

Thus, like rumormongering, gossiping has definite functions that might best be understood within the framework of social exchange. The hierarchy of functions is not identical, but the transactional nature of both phenomena is clearly evident. We turn now to a more intensive examination of the part played by the print and electronic media in these processes, and the implications in regard to social responsibilities.

seven : : Rumor and Gossip in Mass Communications

Rumor and gossip have been the subject of human conversation since man acquired the power of speech. The advent of rapid mass communication has done much to intensify the process, although not long after the turn of the century some had predicted the opposite effect. In 1918, addressing the Royal Historical Society in England, Professor C. W. C. Oman stated [183, pp. 8–12]: "The real death-blow to the long currency of rumours was only dealt in the middle years of the nineteenth century. Since the electric telegraph came in, the rumour in times of peace could never flourish with regard to obvious public events—in a very short time it was discovered whether they had or had not happened."

Because they omitted the human element—"the character of those who direct it," in Bryant's words—reports of the demise of rumor proved premature. The electric telegraph, although a seemingly magical new means of communication, was still merely a channel requiring a human being to determine and direct the flow of content within it.

Little more than a decade after Professor Oman's remarks, bank failures were tangible evidence that his thesis had been incorrect. As masses of people responded to rumors of imminent bank failures by hastily withdrawing their assets, the rumors became self-fulfilling prophecies and bank after bank went under. George Katona writes [130, pp. 659–660]:

> A hundred or even fifty years ago, when news spread slowly and most people were ignorant of happenings outside their limited personal spheres, it was more difficult for incipient recessions and inflations to spread and snowball than it is today. Now with rapid mass communication, every localized difficulty and small price increase becomes generally known and may give rise to mass hysteria.

Barbara Ward, the British economist, notes how electronic communication creates a universal awareness of world events. Satellites speed news around the globe almost instantaneously, creating a global village of gossips. When John Kennedy was assassinated, news of the appalling tragedy was a matter of discussion in remote villages in Africa only hours later. The same had been true several months earlier when Pope John XXIII died. Rumor and gossip follow a similar pattern. Ward notes [254, p. 4]:

> In 1963 . . . my husband was on one of his journeys for the United Nations Special Fund. He went, as I recall it, to India, Malaysia, Ethiopia, Liberia, and Ghana. When he reached home, I said: "Lovely to see you, dear. Tell me about it. How is development getting along? What are they talking about?" His reply was: "Christine Keeler". There you have the village gossip.

DIRECTING THE FLOW OF HEARSAY

Kurt Lewin introduced the concept of the gate-keeper in connection with the channeling and control of group action [152], and the term has been embraced by mass communications researchers to refer more specifically to the news selection behavior of journalists [260]. The print and electronic media have become adept at directing the flow of rumors. Indeed some rumormongering has a news value of sufficient intensity to produce echoes—rumors about the rumormongering. In 1975, Indian Prime Minister Indira Gandhi was tried and found guilty of violating political campaign ethics. Her immediate response to those seeking her resignation was to suspend constitutional rights, impose government censorship on the foreign and domestic press, and to arrest hundreds of her political opponents. On 1 July the *New York Times* reported rumors that anti-Gandhi protesters had been slain, as well as echoes of the intense rumormongering that was rampant—one item stated that there were *rumors* that persons were being arrested in New Delhi for *spreading rumors* about the situation in the capital.

There are several common varieties of rumor that appear in the news media. One type, noted earlier, are stories that are pure fabrications or factoids. An amusing example is the recent Rehoboth pearl hoax, perpetrated by a small weekly newspaper in Delaware [148]. A lead story reported that "Sam (Hobo) Jones," a retired sheet metal worker with a wife named Ethel, had struck it rich when he waded into the surf off Rehoboth Beach and filled two bushel baskets with rare, pearl-laden oysters, described as "meleagrina gargantua, which produce the largest, hardest, most brilliant pearls in the world." The story alleged that Jones found 2–4 high quality pearls in every oyster, each worth from $550 to $1,000. The chief of police, on being informed of the discovery, was reported to have called the Delaware Department of Interior, which in turn contacted the Smithsonian Institute in Washington, D.C., and their Japanese pearl expert, Dr. Laernu Retsyo.

The story was fiction from beginning to end. The pearl expert's name, spelled backwards, revealed a telling clue—"oyster unreal." Hobo Jones, the hero of the tale, was presumably meant to portray the average, middle-class American worker. Unfortunately for those who trekked to Rehoboth Beach to gather in their share of pearl-laden oysters—none could be found outside the active imagination of the prepetrator of the hoax, the editor of the newspaper.

Besides the factoid, another common variety of media rumor

originates in some actual experience and is then propelled by news reports. Not always an eyewitness to events himself, the reporter often arrives on the scene after the fact and interviews sources two or three times removed from the newsworthy happening. Once the story has been written and revised by the reporter and copywriter, leveling, sharpening, and assimilation may have further distorted it [8].

Rumors of coups d'etat or of the illnesses or deaths of great world leaders abound in the print and electronic news media whenever a leader is unexplainably absent on some important state occasion. Recently a popular subject for investigative reporting is the episode in 1969 in which Senator Edward M. Kennedy drove a car off a bridge on Chappaquiddick Island, Massachusetts resulting in the death of Mary Jo Kopechne. For those supporting Kennedy, his behavior has posed a moral dilemma not easily resolved. For those opposed to him, it has reinforced their unfavorable opinions [228]. The result is now a vast and ready audience for both pro- and anti-Kennedy journalists to exploit the situation by resurrecting old rumors.

During the period of the Watergate episode, an ebb and flow of rumors permeated the press, reaching tidal proportions a few days before Nixon's resignation. While they may not have been a direct causative factor in his resignation, these rumors gave voice to the feelings of a majority of the public —according to the Gallup and Harris polls—and amplified those wishes and expectations. On the evening of Nixon's resignation, 8 August 1974, the story that he would actually resign was still unconfirmed by 6 p.m. From 6 p.m. until 9 p.m. Eastern Standard Time (the hour at which Nixon appeared on television) the rumor was being repeated every few minutes by John Chancellor on NBC Television news, which had cancelled all other programs to focus on this important story.

Rumors also frequently appear as front-page news. The juxtaposition of hard news alongside sensationalistic rumors gives the latter credibility by association. Consider the following stories, which appeared in November 1973, on the front pages of two highly respected London newspapers.

The *Guardian* printed an item under the title, "Ghostly Ban," which stated: "A British psychic research newspaper has dropped a report of 'ghostly happenings' in Ireland at the request of the Repbulic's security forces." The item went on to quote the editor of the research newspaper: "The whole thing is extraordinary. We have been told that this story, if it got out, could be exploited by terrorists." In retrospect the innuendo is amusing, but it was not so funny at the time. Londoners were living in an atmosphere of apprehension charged by reading daily accounts of letter bombs and indiscriminate terrorist activity.

During the same period, while American newspapers were featuring all the latest Watergate gossip as front-page news, the London *Times* published a front-page report entitled, "Bonn silent on postal germs story." The story alleged: "A mad scientist is threatening to bombard leading West German politicians with dangerous germs by post unless the Government pays [8 million dollars] according to a macabre rumour circulating in Bonn today." The episode was first reported by BBC Television, then was picked up by a newspaper in Cologne before it made the front page of the *Times*. The report in the *Times*, datelined Bonn, went on to state: "This extraordinary story could normally be dismissed as the product of an overworked imagination, but for the even more extraordinary fact that the authorities here are refusing to comment, or even to deny it." Tucked away in a middle paragraph was a good explanation for why there had been no official comment—it was a public holiday in West Germany, and official sources were simply not available.

A third variety of media rumor is that planted for Machiavellian ends. The part played by the print media in planting rumors for Axis propaganda purposes in Germany, Italy, and Japan during World War II is well known. Hitler, relying upon the public's forgetfulness, believed that momentary rumors, whether true or false, could be used to incite partisan action without incurring any long-run boomerang effects. German radio station DEBUNK was an active medium for Nazi propaganda rumors.

Like rumor, gossip is also given a prominent role in mass communications. Magazines, newspapers, radio and television all make a habit of repeating the latest exciting small talk about political, society, professional, and entertainment personalities. In October, 1975, Secretary of State Henry Kissinger's remarks at a private party in Ottawa were accidentally fed into a radio hookup and transmitted to a lounge in the Canadian National Press Club where they were taped by a newspaperwoman. The next day *The Washington Post*, a newspaper which had moralized on Richard Nixon's White House tapes, splashed a front-page story containing tidbits of Kissinger's gossip. The *New York Times* took a more detached view by emphasizing the role played by the *Post*, but did manage to report the same juicy tidbits, although on page three.

The celebrities and stories may be different when reported in the *Post*, the *London* or *New York Times, People, Newsweek, The New Yorker, Village Voice, Town and Country, Vogue*, and *Parade*, but it constitutes gossip all the same. *Parade* magazine regularly publishes a question-and-answer column giving "the facts", "the truth", "informed opinion" about "prominent personalities"—

> What is the true story of Cher Bono's role in a Hollywood drug party? . . . Whenever Dr. Kissinger flies anywhere, his plane is preceded by another carrying a limousine. Isn't the cost of such luxury outrageous? . . . Is it true that Hugh Hefner of *Playboy* magazine is the secret owner of the famous Masters-Johnson sex clinic in St. Louis? . . . Dean Martin's ex-wife, Jeanne—hasn't she fallen in love with singer Andy Williams? . . . It has long been rumored in Africa that General Idi Amin of Uganda suffers from tertiary syphilis and softening of the brain. Is there any way of verifying this? (*Parade* 20 April 1975)

Gossip and rumor appear in and out of the media—on talk shows, in syndicated columns, and in their ultimate transformation in fiction and drama. The open-microphone radio forum thrives by satisfying a complex of needs [53, 253]. Gossiping is essentially the dramaturgical format of the novel, the motion picture, and the play, which reflect but often ludicrously exaggerate real life. The soap opera is the ultimate caricature. It has cultivated gossiping to such a degree that now soap operas have achieved the status of a modern art form, receiving annual recognition and awards from the entertainment industry.

SOCIAL IMPLICATIONS

These examples are interesting to social psychologists for
what they reveal about society and the practices of journalists
within the culture. The use of sensationalistic phrases such as
"ghostly ban" and "mad scientist" are clearly in contrast with
the American stereotype of the staid British press. To some,
the Watergate stories seem pale in comparison.

It is argued that there is a basic difference between the
treatment accorded political rumors in the British and American press. Because of stricter libel laws in Britain, and the re-
ticence of the British to dwell on unpleasantries, there is
thought to be a tendency for the non-tabloid press to gloss
over most political scandals. Daniel S. Greenberg, an American journalist, was a correspondent in London for several
years. Writing in the London *Observer Magazine* (9 December
1973) at the time of Watergate, he offered the following opinion:

> ... the British Press is mainly focused on fine reporting and keen
> analysis of Governmental *fait accompli,* rather than, as with the
> American Press, advance notice of what the Government would
> rather you didn't know. The best American journalists proceed from
> the horrid assumption that official lying is an integral part of the
> political process, and a principal function of the Press is to lift the
> rocks and spotlight the vermin. If officialdom had been believed,
> neither Watergate nor My Lai would have come to light. If either of
> these scandals had been British productions, the first would have
> been blacked out by legal writs and the second by the Official Se-
> crets Act.

If the leading British press is loathe to flaunt domestic political scandal (which must be a debatable conclusion for anyone
recalling the Profumo affair of 1963 or the recent sex scandal
which led to the resignation of the leader of Britain's Liberal
Party, Jeremy Thorpe), they have shown little reluctance in
featuring other domestic and foreign incidents of a sensational
nature. The London *Times* ("The Times Diary," 10 December
1973) once puckishly called for nominations for the best scare

news of the week. The award that week went to the London *Express* for a rumor about Russian spies slipping into Britain through a Left-wing faction in the Irish Republican Army. The *Express* sheepishly excised the item from later editions of the paper, but by that time the BBC had also reported it. The *Times'* own front-page story of the "mad scientist of Bonn" would have been a close contender in any competition.

Objective and Subjective Inaccuracies in News Reporting

Stories such as these may represent truth, but not the whole truth or balanced truth. As Allport and Postman note [8, p. 187]: "A somewhat distorted picture inevitably results, and when the reader recalls or retells the item he is likely to sharpen it still more in the direction in which it was first slanted". When there are important inaccuracies in the item itself, the problem will be compounded.

Communication researchers Lawrence and Grey have recently discussed two general classes of inaccuracies in news reporting—deviations from the facts or "truth" of an event (objective inaccuracies) and misrepresentations of meaning, completeness, or emphasis (subjective inaccuracies) [147]. Subjective inaccuracies are often more difficult to deal with inasmuch as what appears to be an error of meaning, omission, or emphasis can be a matter of opinion. Indeed the problem appears to be exacerbated whenever there is a lack of communication between the reporter and the news source, which increases the chance for serious subjective inaccuracies to occur. Lawrence and Grey list three safeguards against subjective inaccuracy: (a) reporters should question their news sources about the significance of the event, (b) reporters should be granted ample time to gather background information, particularly if they are unfamiliar with the story, and (c) reporters and editors should cooperate in checking the accuracy of the final report.

Max Hall's account of "the great cabbage hoax" illustrates what can happen when writers and editors fail to check the accuracy of an appealing news item, and as a result perpetuate a false rumor [100]. Hall, the Director of Public Information at the Office of Price Stabilization (OPS) in the Truman Administration, was attending a convention of the Southern Garment Manufacturers Association in Memphis, Tennessee in August 1951. In introducing the guest speaker, Michael V. Disalle, head of OPS, the toastmaster repeated a story he'd read: the Gettysberg Address contained 266 words, the Ten Commandments contained 297 words, the Declaration of Independence contained 300 words, but *an OPS directive to regulate the price of cabbage contained 26,911 words.* (The word count for the Declaration of Independence carried an unnoticed inaccuracy, but more importantly, the cabbage story was a complete fabrication. OPS had no regulation devoted exclusively to cabbage. In fact, it was an old tale that had been circulating in the 1940s about the Office of Price Administration (OPA).

The cabbage rumor aroused the displeasure of OPS officials, who sought to quash it. By this time, however, it had gathered momentum. On the following day it appeared in the *New York Daily News,* in the form of a letter from someone in North Bergen, New Jersey. Two weeks later it was repeated in a circular mimeographed on the letterhead of a Chicago pickle producer, with a citation to the Grocery Manufacturers of America. Soon the rumor became a routine item in press and radio news reports. Some editorial writers poked fun at the OPS; others used the story as a basis for ridiculing the Truman Administration, the federal bureaucracy, and Washington politicians in general. The *Saturday Evening Post* noted in an editorial that "some socialist-minded Washingtonians tried to give the Muscovites a run for their rubles", but the Americans never had a chance because a factory in Siberia received a questionnaire of 1,487,400 questions from the Kharkov Institute of Fire Bricks—an espisode "sure to bring a blush of shame to the cheeks of our OPS."

The cabbage joke was mentioned by Morgan Beatty on NBC radio news. Beatty, who reported having gotten the item from the *Wall Street Journal,* later apologized when he was informed that the story was a hoax. He corrected the report the next night on the radio, chiding the *Journal* for not having checked the item's accuracy. The newspapers also corrected their errors, but by this time the denials were unable to catch up with the rumor. On the NBC quiz show, "Double or Nothing", the "grand-slam" question put to the contestants was to

guess how many words were contained in an OPS order to reduce the price of cabbage. Notified of this incident by a radio
listener, OPS contacted the master of ceremonies, Dennis
O'Keefe, who then referred the matter to the program's spon-
sor, the Campbell Soup Company. Their decision was not to
correct the error because it was "bad business to try to publicize such mistakes." Instead, they promised to send an as-
sorted case of Campbell soup to the alert listener who had
contacted OPS.

In only one instance did an editor apparently bother to verify the item. When this person learned that the cabbage order
did not exist, he merely substituted another commodity,
"manually operated foghorns." This time there was some truth
to the news report, although it neglected to mention that the
foghorn directive was a comprehensive order referring to some
376 manufactured items. The cabbage rumor persisted in the
press for several years, providing entertainment and emotional
satisfaction for the public and an opportunity for writers and
editors to poke fun at the federal bureaucracy.

SOCIAL RESPONSIBILITY

Few reporters or editors would tamper with information
coming from authoritative sources. However, that does not
preclude their patterning the news reports to their own viewpoints and value orientations. In a well known study in mass
communications research, Allport and Faden conducted a content analysis of Boston newspapers in 1939, at the time Congress was considering the Neutrality Act [7]. They found that,
for the majority of papers surveyed, news items favoring the
editorial policy of the paper received more space. Supportive
facts and opinions were placed at the beginning of a news article, opposing facts and opinions were placed at the end. Allport and Postman later commented [8, p. 187]: "This sly
editorial device served to level out in the reader's mind the
disfavored view and to sharpen the favored."

Rumors, having none of the concreteness of hard news, can
more easily be shaped to conform to a particular point of view.
In another well known study, undertaken shortly after V-E

Day in 1945, Elizabeth H. Zerner analyzed the content of 30 Paris daily newspapers to determine whether they were selectively printing rumors agreeable to their political attitudes [268]. She studied the appearance of one set of rumors in particular, pertaining to the illness of Soviet leader Josef Stalin. Although only some of these newspapers openly represented a political group or party, the attitude of each was known well enough to classify all 30 by their pro- or anti-Communist leanings. A variety of rumors appeared in the newspapers over the four month period of the investigation. They included such items as confirmations and denials of Stalin's illness or death, speculations on his successor, and rumors of a political crisis in Russia. Zerner found a definite relationship between the ideological slants of the newspapers and the content of the rumors printed. Anti-Communist papers stressed Stalin's illness and a crisis in Russia; pro-Communist papers either ignored these subjects or carried rumors denying the allegations. Hence, we observe that the attitude and value orientations of journalists can affect the configuration of the news reported.

There is also evidence of a high degree of philosophical conformity in the news selection values of reporters (but a difference in emphasis with regard to the importance of news as judged by the public versus the judgments of editors) [14, 15, 101]. The reporter first learns value expectations from those who teach him his craft, and the socialization process continues throughout his practice of journalism ultimately being redefined according to the pragmatic level of his publisher and professional colleagues [cf. 14, 28, 29, 44, 64, 89, 96]. One result of this homogenization of news selection values may be the kind of bias noted in the cases given above, in which a small professional elite addresses a widely dispersed and heterogeneous audience [101].

The inherent hazard derives from the circumstance that public access to the news media is drastically skewed in favor of the media. Feedback is weak, unorganized, and generally ineffective. Equally important is that media content is a pacesetter for contemporary society as well as a reflector of it. For these reasons, especially, journalists must be sensitive and responsive to societal problems while endeavoring to avoid becoming part of the problems themselves. To be sure, there is a difference of opinion over the degree of influence, intentional or unintentional, exerted by the mass media [168]. Nonetheless, like a divining rod that is oriented to water, the media are by nature oriented to what is novel and dramatic. In their emphasis and selective reporting of newsworthy happenings, they help to fashion a picture of reality and define for others what is important or unimportant. The most popular news medium, television, simultaneously spans distance, telescopes time, and extends man's visual contact with the world. One sees, day by day, the progress of a war, the misery or joy of people in a distant country—this is the true essence of the "global village" referred to by Barbara Ward, for people all over the world are practically face to face with one another [254; cf. 143, p. 167].

Many have suggested that news selection values and certain habits of the media, television in particular, cause them to be essentially implicated in the pattern of events [68, 69, 80, 150; cf. 261]. Jeffrey Goldstein points out that there is ample evidence to show the publicity given violent acts contributes to criminal aggression [98]. Conversely, Payne and Payne observed a decrease in criminal activities during a newspaper strike in Detroit, Michigan [187]. Other psychological research implies that reporters (like other non-participating observers), are normally more attuned to events and environmental circumstances than to the motivations of the persons involved in the events, and will therefore tend to form impressions giving greater weight to situational elements than to individual emotional states or intentions [257]. Terry Ann Knopf [141], who has made an extensive study of rumors and riots, assumes the radical stance in arguing that the American news media needlessly increase racial tensions by presenting a distorted view of reality that aims to justify rather than to explain events. Somewhat in contrast to Daniel Greenberg's analysis, political scientist Bernard Rubin argues that the electronic media treat news in the extreme, either as dramatic and provocative or as undramatic and of little importance [217]. It is difficult to separate information from entertainment, hard fact from rumor, significant information from gossip—which "conditions" the public to a superficial level of cognition. American television is event-happy, Rubin maintains; it focuses on the figure and ignores the ground, never going behind the facade of news events to learn what is *really* happening. However, the media may also be caught in a double-bind, for when they stand above a problem and judge it impartially, the public (which is encouraged to identify with the presenter) may come to see itself as a neutral and dispassionate spectator of partisan and impassioned conflict, and thus be reluctant to take an active hand in social change for the betterment of humanity [101].

The issues of social responsibility and accountability are extremely complicated and profound. Journalists must be responsive to events in a more than voyeuristic sense, but they must also be sensitive to the individual's right to privacy. For obvious practical and philosophical reasons the specter of censorship is an unwelcome visitor. Declaring things taboo enhances their emotional value. In a society with constitutional guarantees to free speech and freedom of the press, both the public and the press must keep watch to guard against infringements on the lawful and moral rights both of the individual and society.

eight :: Control of Rumor and Gossip

Let the greatest part of the news thou hearest be the least part of what thou believest, lest the greater part of what thou believest be the least part of what is true.

FRANCIS QUARLES
Enchyridion

In August 1971 hurricane Dora pounded the East Coast of the United States, lashing the Middle Atlantic states with heavy rains for several days. She flooded railroad tracks in parts of New Jersey causing frustrated train travelers, seeking alternate transportation, to descend on interstate bus terminals in large numbers. The queues grew longer and longer as the record storm flooded parts of the New Jersey Turnpike and the Garden State Expressway, bringing automobile traffic to a standstill. In Philadelphia's Greyhound Bus Terminal bogie rumors spread from person to person. There were tales of the high toll of fatalities, the utter devastation of the Turnpike, and the closing of Philadelphia Airport. The rumors were contagious products of uncontrolled imaginations, as in fact there were no highway deaths due to the flooding, the damage to the Turnpike was minimal and temporary, and airplanes were not only operating but on schedule. The rumors had gathered momentum in the collective wish for information and security, and collective feelings of anxiety were responsible for their dissemination. The more people who passed on the rumor, the easier it was to believe.

In such a situation rumors will continue until the underlying collective needs are fulfilled or the anxieties alleviated. However, there are other circumstances where human needs are never fully gratified and are therefore perpetually sensitive to outbreaks of rumor.

PERSISTENT SENSITIVITIES

One such need, affecting all of us who live in this age of rapid mass communication, is the unquenchable desire for news. The sensation of future shock in a rapidly evolving post-industrial society creates a yearning for closure, stability, certainty, and a strong orientation to learn what is new. If we, as consumers of news, hunger for the latest information, the journalist's appetite for the novel, the bizarre, and the unexplained is insatiable. It is no wonder tales such as the one concerning the mad scientist of Bonn or that of the great cabbage hoax receive prominent news coverage. Nor is it surprising that reporters develop a keen sensitivity to ambiguities and unexplained incidents.

In early 1975 rumors proliferated in the world press about Soviet Party Leader, Leonid Brezhnev, who had not been seen in public for five weeks. In various accounts "informed sources" stated he was suffering from no fewer than twenty-one ailments ranging in seriousness from a bad toothache to leukemia. One intriguing factoid, which initially appeared in the *Boston Globe*, stated that he was enroute to Massachusetts to be treated at a world-famous cancer clinic. It was later disclosed that the rumor had been prompted by a prankster who fed information into the clinic's computer, listing "L. Brezhnev" as an incoming patient. Both the *Globe* and the Boston Police Department were "tipped off" simultaneously. When the *Globe*, failing to get a flat denial from Washington, heard the identical rumor from a police source, they rushed the story into print.

Another curious illustration revolves around the English Channel and the so-called "chunnel", referring to a theoretical tunnel under this body of water which separates Southern England and Northern France. Throughout modern history, whenever Englishmen have sensed a threat to the natural insularity of their island fortress, chunnel rumors have surfaced.

A famous outbreak of chunnel rumors occurred during the Napoleonic Period of the early 19th century. The tale held that the French were planning to invade England by burrowing mole-like under the Channel. A line-engraving done in France around 1803 depicts the imaginary French invasion by balloons, ships, and underground infantry (FIG. 14). Remarkably, a

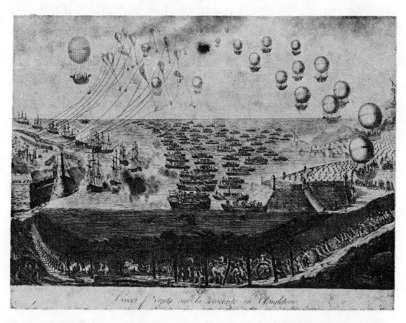

FIGURE 14. Chunnel rumors have surfaced throughout modern history whenever Englishmen have sensed a threat to the natural insularity of their island fortress. In this line-engraving, circa 1803, the Napoleonic French are depicted as raiding England by air, sea, and chunnel. (*Photograph courtesy of Bibliothèque Nationale, Paris*)

similar rumor sprouted during World War II: the Germans, having failed to subdue England from the air after Dunkirk, were now tunneling under the Channel for a surprise invasion!

The British Government immediately undertook scientific experiments in the detection of undersea digging, and authorized regular reconnaissance flights over suspected sites along the French coast. It was not until detection experiments with "quartz piezo electric accelerometers" were proven successful that the secret file was finally closed [177].

In the late 1800s, and again in the 1960s and 1970s, new chunnel stories sprang up when efforts were actually made to construct an underground tunnel as a railway link between Britain and Europe. Rumors circulated about I.R.A. sabotage plans, disastrous leaks, and watery graves. In 1973 when the economic recession caused Britain to discontinue the construction begun near Dover, the rumors also terminated—perhaps in hibernation until the plan is revived. The celebrated English cartoonist, W. Heath Robinson, has immortalized the bogie rumor about a leak in the chunnel in his marvelous cartoon depicting a school of fish gaping in wonderment as some modern-day Hans Brinker uses his head to plug the hole (FIG. 15).

These examples teach us that one can treat a rumor, but not always its etiology. Some areas can be regarded almost as an "Achilles heel", perpetually sensitive to the slightest stimulation. Because there are no effective solutions for rendering them invulnerable to rumormongering, the result is often a treatment of symptoms rather than causes. However, there are measures which may act as deterrents against damaging or malicious rumors and gossip.

PREVENTIVE MEASURES

The obvious deterrents are legal sanctions, prohibitions, and censorship. When tourist-minded officials in Malaysia sought to end rumors that headhunters were roaming North Borneo, the chief government minister, Abdul Rahman Yaacob, announced "big cash rewards" to those with information leading to arrests of rumormongers (Associated Press, 7 March 1973). In a similar vein, several years before the Communist takeover of South Vietnam, the South Vietnamese Government announced that it would enforce a law providing penalties rang-

FIGURE 15. The English artist W. Heath Robinson immortalized the rumor about leaks in the chunnel in this cartoon showing a modern-day Hans Brinker using his head to plug a hole. *(Reproduced courtesy of the Estate of the late W. Heath Robinson and the publisher)*

ing from ten years in jail to death for spreading rumors harmful to the national economy (Associated Press, 19 November 1971).

The U.S. Criminal Code (Title 18, Section 1009) states that making, circulating, or transmitting any untrue derogatory rumor about the financial standing of the Federal Savings and Loan Corporation will be subject to possible fine and imprisonment. Many states have enacted similar legislation against bogie financial rumors. In Alaska, circulation of a rumor of this type constitutes a felony punishable by a fine of up to $5,000 and a prison term up to five years (Alaska Statutes, 1974, Title 6, Sec. 06.05.505.). Other states have made it a crime to spread derogatory rumors about credit unions and agricultural co-operatives. Most people are aware of the existence of laws against libel, slander, and defamation of character—a subject examined in detail in a later section. This type of legislation which attempts to prevent the public from engaging in certain forms of rumormongering or gossiping is very difficult to enforce, and (except in some special situations) would seem to have only marginal utility. Some argue that the potential infringement on freedom of speech far outweighs the possible benefits.

Sanctions and prohibitions can also backfire by enhancing the psychological value of the prohibited behavior. In December 1970 the American press carried critical reports of curbs imposed by the Greek Government against correspondents "spreading false rumors". Almost immediately, the Royal Greek Embassy Press and Information Service issued an emphatic and categorical denial that curbs had been imposed on foreign correspondents. The statement failed to mention whether sanctions had been imposed (or subsequently lifted) on Greek nationals. The denial and innuendo became worthy news items in their own right, generating further speculations by the press, radio, and television.

It is self-evident that prohibitions can be effective only if they are credible and enforceable and we shall return to this point subsequently. However, by the time a situation requires enforcement of prohibitions, the damage will be done. In 1970 the American Stock Exchange disciplined two of its floor members for rumormongering on the condition of a financially troubled brokerage firm. On the afternoon of 25 November rumors swept Wall Street when the firm announced that it would make a statement concerning its financial condition at 4:30 p.m. The purpose of the statement was to quell conjectures by reporting that the firm had received a $15-million capital infusion. Before that statement could be issued, a rumor suddenly surfaced that certain wealthy members of the firm were planning to withdraw substantial amounts of capital, which would require the firm to liquidate. The opposite was true: they had added to the capital of the firm. AMEX fined the two known rumormongers $1,000 each and reminded all members of Rule 3c.

There has also been exploratory research done on preventing rumormongering by heightening one's awareness of its occurrence and potentially damaging effects. Previously we discussed Allport and Postman's laboratory simulations of rumormongering which consisted of having persons transmit an "eyewitness" account of a richly detailed social situation seen on a slide. By analyzing the individual accounts in the serial chain of communication, the processes of leveling, sharpening, and assimilation were identified. The identical procedure was employed by June Tapp in the early 1950s to sensitize children to the nature of malicious rumormongering [243, 244]. By this device she sought to teach how rumors based on stereotypes can act as substitutes for careful observation and create social strains by raising false hopes, spreading fear and apprehension, building hostilities, and driving emotional wedges between people.

Tapp prepared an elaborate slide depicting a number of social situations familiar to the sixth-graders in her study. The slide showed a cluster of people conversing outside a church while a plane flies overhead, two couples standing beside a house with a "For Rent" sign on it, a man standing next to an open car and exchanging something with a little girl, six children on a baseball diamond watching as a white adolescent boy holds a baseball and interacts with a black adolescent boy holding a baseball bat. Tapp selected five students in each participating classroom, and designated the students "reporters". As the class observed, one reporter was summoned into the classroom and shown the slide. Then a second reporter was told by the first reporter everything he or she could remember about the complicated picture. Reporter 2 passed this information to reporter 3, and so on, until all reporters had been informed of what the "eyewitness" had seen. At the conclusion of the study the children discussed transcripts made from tape recordings of what each reporter had said contrasted with what the eyewitness had seen, the nature of rumors and rumormongering, and how they thought malicious rumors could be combatted. Unfortunately, no data were collected in regard to long-term effects, but Tapp did observe that the children seemed to become more rumor conscious, evidenced by their ability to notice instances of rumor distortions.

Other promising strategies which merit further exploration derive from recent social psychological research programs on inducing resistance to persuasion. The best known of these is the research of William J. McGuire and his associates at Yale University, based on the biological analogy of inoculation [165]. McGuire conducted an impressive series of experiments in which cultural truisms were the focal issues (for example "brushing your teeth after every meal is good for your health"). Because such beliefs go virtually unchallenged in our culture, they can be said to exist almost in a "germ free" psychological environment. They should, therefore, be highly vulnerable to "germs" in the form of logical arguments. To prevent truisms from becoming overly influenced by prop-agandistic arguments, McGuire attempted to bolster a person's defenses by exposure to similar arguments in advance of a germ attack—thereby stimulating the production of antibodies in the form of counterarguments. If the analogy can be generalized to the problem of warding off the effects of poten-tially harmful bogie and wedge-driving rumors, the research question becomes that of establishing the exact amount of counterargumentation needed to build a person's defenses without actually infecting him by the counterarguments them-selves.

In a similar vein, the research of social psychologist Percy H. Tannenbaum has experimented with alternate methods of increasing resistance to persuasion [242]. In contrast to the in-oculation model of McGuire, Tannenbaum's research has pro-ceeded from the psychological principle that attitude change is a direct consequence of cognitive incongruity. The situation considered by Tannenbaum was when someone (favorably re-garded) is represented as having made a negative remark about a person or issue (also favorably regarded). For example, sup-pose you heard a rumor that a classified report of the U.S. Pub-lic Health Service asserts that brushing your teeth after every meal is dangerous to your health because it destroys beneficial organisms in the mouth. The combination of a positive source (the Public Health Service) issuing a negative assertion (too much brushing can be harmful) about a positive concept (con-scientious oral hygiene) sets up an incongruity, which according to the theory should lead to a shift in attitude that brings the combination of valences into balance. If one's pattern of oral hygiene was altered, this would in effect return all to a balanced state (but not a desirable one from a medical standpoint). Tannenbaum posed the question: how to eliminate or reduce this negative shift in attitude. Extensive experimentation found four effective procedures, which appear to have a cumulative ameliorative effect when used in combination —denial of the assertion, derogation of the source, logical refutation of the assertion, and strengthening the original concept through counterargumentation.

In the final section of this chapter we now discuss the control and treatment of rumor and gossip in regard to four general cases, applying what is known about (a) rumor in times of political turmoil, (b) rumor during natural disaster, (c) rumor in wartime or in times of extended racial tension, and (d) defamatory gossip and rumor aimed at individuals. These general circumstances do not exhaust all cases in which controls might properly be employed. They do, however, present a representative range of circumstances, each with its own special problems, from personal issues to questions of the continuation of the state.

POLITICAL TURMOIL

Let us consider as an example of an extreme political crisis the immediate aftermath of an assassination. Rumors abound. Everyone has an opinion on the motive and perpetrators of the crime: it was a conspiracy; it was a madman acting alone. In the assassination of John Kennedy it was not clear, despite films and still photographs of the crime, how he was shot. The resulting controversy fueled many speculative rumors which are still going strong. The assassination of Robert Kennedy was reported as the work of a deranged person. Rumors sprang up quickly that others were involved, and in 1975 (seven years after the senator's death) the case was reopened by the Los Angeles Police Department.

A key factor to be considered in deciding how to treat bogie and other potentially harmful rumors in these circumstances is the amount of trust that citizens have in their government and in the news media. In a modern industrial society news is disseminated with remarkable speed. But these news stories often ignore or gloss over details and individual motivations. In a society with a free and divided press, different sources may contradict each other—which must inevitably add to the confusion and increase feelings of anxiety and fear. A free press also allows those with an ax to grind to do their mischief.

The goals of the government in a national crisis are to calm the populace, to restore and maintain faith in the orderly processes of government, and to make available accurate information as quickly as possible. If there is good faith, the problems will be less severe than if there has been a history of distrust and suspicion. At the time John Kennedy was killed, there was public trust in the government and press. Most people, initially, were ready to accept reports of the crime as revealed by the Dallas police and the F.B.I. Later on, however, many people began to entertain grave doubts as to whether the evidence was legitimate and the conclusions reached the correct ones. Today, in the aftermath of Watergate, calls are being made for a reopening of the Warren Commission's investigation, as now the possibility of C.I.A. or Cuban murder plots against Kennedy are given credence by a wider segment of the population. It is fair to say that if a similar tragic episode occurred at this moment, the Federal government would have a very difficult time convincing the American public of the "facts" of the case.

Thus, before choosing a strategy (for example, those tried by Tannenbaum in his research on increasing resistance) the general temperament and past experiences of the community must be given careful attention. The typical resources available to a government or controlling agency will consist of media and fact-gathering bodies. The government usually controls the fact-gathering organizations directly, and it exerts some control on the media directly or indirectly. In addition, the government has enforcement agencies, so that control can be forcibly maintained if necessary. This forcible control, though possibly effective for preventing some violence and panic, will have little positive impact on preventing bogie rumors. It is impossible to stop private free speech by brute force entirely, although force may have a chilling effect on public speech. More effective will be trusted officials revealing trustworthy news.

Many studies of attitude change have shown that to achieve a strong positive effect it is necessary for the source of information to be perceived as highly credible [215]. This stipulation is especially important in a political crisis, and reintroduction of the source can be effective in countering a possible sleeper effect [133]. The research reveals five basic dimensions of source credibility which ought to be considered —expertness, reliability, intentions, dynamism, and attractiveness [90]. Expertness is a combination of authoritativeness, perceived intelligence, and certain nonverbal factors. Because the expert is seen as having the facts and the skilled judgment to reinterpret them accurately, he or she is viewed as trustworthy. Reliability has to do with how the source is perceived in terms of a person's value system. Being thought dependable and consistent in one's judgment will convey an image of high credibility. The source's intentions and motivations constitute a third factor. It is important that the source is not seen to unfairly profit by any recommendations, particularly if he has not set an example by his own behavior. Two factors having lesser influence are the source's dynamism (or activity level) and his persuasiveness. Any of these five basic dimensions can come into play when there is an active attempt to quash a rumor by issuing government denials regarding the substance of the story.

NATURAL DISASTER

Most situations which produce rumors are not national in scope. In the aftermath of a local emergency, people will still seek information and advice from credible sources, and the dimensions of source credibility are important then as well.

People may have heard, for example, about a raging forest fire threatening them, or the possibility of a flood, dam-break, or earthquake. As in a national political crisis, there may be a strong potential for panic or physical damage to persons or property. The problem in this case is how best to communicate useful information, since the same mass media approach used to treat national emergencies may not be adequate in isolated areas without full access to the media or in situations where power lines are down.

The objectives of control agencies will be to prevent damage and panic, goals which can probably be achieved by the quick dissemination of vital information. If authorities have access to radio and television, and can saturate the airwaves with facts and guidance, panic often can be averted. However, other channels of communication might also be used in an emergency—pamphlets dropped from planes, helicopter-based loudspeakers, and public meetings with community opinion leaders. It is vitally important for people to have access to informed, trusted authorities. One factor producing panic in the aftermath of the invasion from Mars broadcast in 1938 was that telephone lines to the police were tied up, and even those who got through often found that the police knew no more than they did [37]. Long before an emergency occurs, all agencies concerned with civil defense and public safety should consider and rehearse ways of dealing with damaging rumors, and these plans should be regularly reviewed. If there is ample warning of a local emergency (a storm warning, for example) residents should be fully advised of what to expect and how to cope with the impending peril.

The crisis arising from a natural disaster is the one situation in rumor control in which the truth of the refutation is not of crucial importance. It is essential, however, that the advice given be appropriate. This is not to suggest that officials should knowingly lie, only that there may be some cases where facts are better slanted or omitted in order to prevent panic or to keep the peace [cf. 129, p. 551]. In a panic in a crowded theater, if the audience learned the real extent of the danger, a disorderly exit might result in needless loss of life; whereas if they are convinced that it was a minor incident, all might safely escape [225]. Public safety officials have keeping people alive as their first priority, and they must take whatever sensible steps are necessary to accomplish this.

PERIODS OF EXTENDED STRESS

Rumors in wartime or during a period of extended racial conflict can have serious, even fatal, consequences. In a major work in this area, Terry Ann Knopf traces the influence of rumors in racial tension to the very beginnings of our nation [141]. In 1741 rumors in colonial New York concerned suspicious fires supposedly set by slaves. By the Civil War racial rumors were rife, and during the 20th century rumors have accompanied, and often preceded or provoked, every major instance of racial violence. As noted earlier, the Kerner Commission estimated that rumors significantly aggravated tension and disorder in approximately two-thirds of the disorders studied [136]. Gordon Allport went further in claiming [6, p. 61] that "no riot or lynching ever occurs without the aid of rumor." These rumors can build animosity and thus serve as a barometer of tensions in the community. They can be the spark which ignites violence. Rumors in a stressful situation will sustain the excitement and may even intensify it. Indeed, the mere repetition of rumors may indicate to some that they are accurate or that there is a kernel of truth in them [182].

Public officials, including the police and internal security forces, have important responsibilities in dealing with the population during a period of extended stress. They must be careful not to let themselves become the source of rumors. Knopf cites the role of New York Mayor Fiorello LaGuardia in spreading rumors by claiming that the 1943 Harlem riots were the doing of criminals and hoodlums [141, pp. 54–55]. Public officials must be accountable to the population and certain that the information they provide is accurate. To deal effectively with riots and other civil disturbances, the police and agencies of control must be trained in community relations—rather than approaching the problem without special competence or organized procedures.

Rumor Control Centers

During the 1960s the rumor control center was developed as an institutional mechanism for combatting malicious rumor-mongering, an idea which derived from World War II rumor clinics. The late Gordon Allport, professor of psychology at Harvard University, is credited with having inspired the first rumor clinic, established in Boston shortly after the outbreak of the Second World War [139]. Others who significantly contributed to the formation of the Boston Rumor Clinic were Robert H. Knapp, then a graduate student at Harvard who was working for his Ph.D. under Allport, and Frances Sweeney, a civic-minded woman.

According to an account published in *American Mercury* magazine in 1942 [162], Frances Sweeney became disheartened by the large number of anti-Semitic, anti-British, and defeatist rumors which were current in certain sectors of the Boston Irish community, and she helped to arrange a meeting of public officials and other local leaders to plan a campaign for counteracting these malicious tales. Shortly before the meeting, the Queen Mary docked at Boston Harbor for a few days. Although local newspapers agreed not to mention the ship's presence, it soon became public knowledge and the object of intense rumormongering. At this first meeting each person recalled the stories he or she had heard in connection with the ship's visit. The police commissioner told of a rumor circulating in the black community that the Queen Mary was crammed with Negro troops destined for suicide missions. Someone from a local college reported a rumor that there was not a single Jew aboard, that all the Jewish soldiers had managed to evade overseas duty. A social worker present mentioned having heard that the ship had gone out of Boston Harbor ablaze from stem to stern. A businessman said that the ship had sunk not far from Boston with great loss of American life. Someone else had heard a rumor about a mutiny aboard ship.

The rich variety of these stories convinced all present of the need to organize a city-wide effort to combat rumormongering, and Knapp was put in charge of the Division of Propaganda Research responsible for tracking down and refuting false tales. It came to be known as the Rumor Clinic, and a weekly column under that name began to appear in the Boston *Herald*. The organization of the Clinic included an advisory board made up of psychology professors, journalists, union representatives, members of ethnic and religious groups, and law-enforcement officials. There were also "rumor-wardens" and "morale-wardens", volunteers selected because their occupations made them particularly well suited as repositories of rumor. The local bartenders union helped to enlist more than 200 morale-wardens to report rumors. Besides the weekly newspaper column which provided a detailed refutation of false rumors the Clinic also distributed pamphlets and posters on the subject of rumormongering and read bulletins at union meetings. Frances Sweeney spent much of her time tracking down stories, and as a result was able to identify the propagandistic nature of many bogie and wedge-driving rumors. Knapp's experiences led him to develop six general guidelines in dealing with malicious rumor [139, pp. 35–36]:

(a) Assure good faith in the regular media of communication so that people can rely on the news media for complete and accurate information.
(b) Develop confidence and faith in leaders which will help the public to abide the frustrations of censorship and inadequate information at a time when the air is poisoned by suspicion and distrust.
(c) Issue as much news as quickly as possible in order to fill the vacuum of ambiguity with reliable information.
(d) Make reliable information and authoritative interpretation readily accessible in order that false tales be quickly and easily refuted.
(e) Try to prevent idleness, monotony, and personal disorganization as they lead to psychological conditions which are highly conducive to rumormongering and gossiping.
(f) Campaign deliberately against rumormongering by showing its harmful effects, its inaccuracies, and the low motives of the originators and liaisons of such tales.

From this early effort evolved the rumor control centers which have operated sporadically in this country in recent years. The prototype of these modern "rumor clinics" was organized in Chicago in 1967. As of 1974 there were 36 rumor centers still in operation in cities of over 100,000 population, and Knopf cites a total of 97 cities with experience with rumor control centers.

Most researchers have found that these centers are helpful in preventing or reducing disorder as well as in putting a stop to malicious rumor and gossip [136, 172, 193, 262]. However, some doubt the effectiveness of rumor control centers, pointing out that they do not really deal with the problems behind the disorders, but only with symptoms [142]. A more serious criticism is that most rumor centers reach only one segment of the population—in the case of racial incidents, reaching white *or* black, rarely both. Chicago Rumor Central was used primarily by white residents; it provided little service to blacks. This is an issue that is difficult to resolve, because obviously no one can be forced to call a rumor center for advice, and the distrust has evolved from years of suspicion.

One innovative, yet largely unplanned, way of dealing with this issue occurred in Boston during the attempts to desegregate the Boston public schools. In the summer of 1974, the U.S. District Court ruled that Boston would have to desegregate its public schools that autumn through massive busing—a decree that was bound to, and did, have severe and traumatic repercussions for the city. In dealing with the problem, Information Centers developed to provide parents with news about the schools and also to handle any disorders which might arise. Because the city was fragmented, and there was sufficient time for planning responses to disorders, a number of groups evolved to deal with the varying segments of the population. Over a dozen groups eventually operated, a situation with virtues as well as drawbacks. The organizations sponsoring information included the Mayor's Office (politically moderate, with a determination that the court's order be administered), the Boston School Committee (anti-busing, but compelled to carry out the order of the court), Freedom House (a black community information service, pro-desegregation and in favor of the court's order), and a number of local information centers in the various neighborhoods of Boston, including the most troubled area, South Boston (vehemently anti-busing). Information Centers were even established in a few Boston suburbs.

This complex situation led to considerable confusion, as not all groups had access to the same information. The South Boston Information Center admits to unintentionally passing on erroneous information on occasion. In some cases there was rivalry and political friction between groups, most notably between City Hall and the School Committee. However, no matter what a person's political orientation, everyone at least had a source for confirmation or denial of rumors. The goal of all the centers was the dissemination of accurate information about the schools and the prevention of violence. Even the South Boston group felt that they helped to keep the community quiet, particularly in the aftermath of a racially motivated stabbing of a white student. It is impossible to be certain of the effect of these centers, because we have no way of knowing what the situation would have been like without them. However, inasmuch as they did at least attempt to provide accurate information, had a sincere desire to be of service, and provided a place for people to let off steam, we endorse the concept as one means of serving the community.

For the reader interested in the specifics of establishing a rumor control center, the Appendix contains a list of standards and guidelines developed by the Community Relations Service of the U.S. Department of Justice.

DEFAMATORY GOSSIP AND RUMOR

Although defamatory gossip and rumor aimed at individuals may not have the same impact on society that bogie and wedge-driving rumors have, these forms are also capable of causing great pain. Imagine rumors about your income splashed across the front page of the local newspaper, or suppose you are a small manufacturer whose products are called worthless on national television. Most probably you would demand compensation or even retribution for this defamatory gossip or rumor which you consider libel or slander.

In the United States laws of libel and slander are not national but are part of the states' criminal and civil codes. This means that in some states the penalties for speaking ill of another are more harsh than others. A person who has been libeled by a television network may choose to bring action in *any* of the jurisdictions where the defamation was broadcast, or may sue in several locales. Penalties, statutes of limitations, full and partial defenses vary state by state, making any general remarks on this subject possibly invalid for individual states.

Words tending to expose an individual to hatred, contempt, or ridicule, or to deprive him of business, public confidence, or social intercourse, are considered actionable. That is, they are grounds for a libel or slander suit. For example, it is actionable in Georgia to impute that a white female has had sexual intercourse "with a person of color" (Code of Georgia Annotated, Title 105–107, 1968). Many states consider accusing a woman of being unchaste not only unchivalrous, but actionable as well. It is actionable in Arkansas, Idaho, Mississippi, Tennessee, West Virginia, and Massachusetts to accuse a person of cowardice for not accepting a duel. Clearly, the charges may vary considerably across jurisdictions.

American libel and slander laws evolved directly from English common law. However, with the development of electronic mass communications, standard legal interpretations have sometimes had to be modified. The old distinction was that libel referred to written or printed defamation, and slander referred to what had been spoken. Libel was judged the more serious offense because of its potential to reach a vast audience and because it was also more likely to be premeditated (as opposed to having been expressed in the heat of the moment). However, radio and television, while using the spoken rather than the printed word, also subject a vast audience to essentially premeditated content. In 1947, in the case of Hartmann versus Winchell, the New York State Court of Appeals ruled that since a particular radio broadcast by Walter Winchell had been read from a script, it constituted libel rather than slander (296 N.Y. 296). A concurring decision stated that all defamatory broadcasts were libelous because of the size of the audience reached. The tendency recently has been to accept this concurring opinion that defamation over the airwaves is libel, and thus stricter rules apply [189].

Recourse to libel suits allows the aggrieved party to institute a civil action for whatever monetary damage occurred to his reputation (compensatory damages) plus an additional amount to set the record straight and to punish the defamer (punitive damages)—the civilized substitute for physical revenge. Generally, compensatory damages are relatively low since they must involve provable monetary loss, while punitive damages can be quite high—to the millions of dollars. In the case of Butts versus Curtis Publishing Co., the jury returned a verdict of $60,000 in compensatory damages and $3,000,000 in punitive damages for the former University of Georgia athletic director who had been accused in the *Saturday Evening Post* of "fixing" a football game with the University of Alabama (225 F. Supp. 916). The judge in reviewing the case reduced the punitive damages to $400,000, the highest amount ever awarded.

For a statement to be defamatory in a legal sense, it must meet three criteria. The statement must be published—that is, communicated to a third party (even to just one other individual). The statement must identify the victimized party—not necessarily by name; circumstances or a nickname will do. Finally, some crime or dishonor must be charged. If all criteria are met, then the statement is judged defamatory and constitutes libel or slander—though not necessarily punishable libel or slander. The defendant has recourse to several possible defenses to show that though the statement is defamatory, he had the right to make it. For example, a legal defense could be made on the basis of local statutes of limitations, the privilege of a participant to an event, the privilege of reporting, the *"New York Times* rule" (see below), fair comment and criticism, consent or authorization, self-defense and right of reply, and truth. The truth does not make a statement non-punishable. Interested readers are referred to their local law or journalism library for further discussion of this and for the somewhat stricter British defamation law [cf. 11, 13, 39, 184, 189, 248].

If the media report an inaccurate defamatory rumor, even if they did not start the story, they are open to a libel suit.

Perhaps this is a necessary corrective for newspapers too anxious to rush into print without sufficient documentary evidence. Libel and slander laws do not abridge freedom of speech or of the press in that they do not *prevent* action; they just demand that responsibility be taken in a civil procedure. (There are criminal laws against libel and slander as well, but these are rarely invoked when a civil suit can be brought.)

To the ultrasensitive eye critical dissent may be misperceived as "libel", and one important purpose of the First Amendment is to protect the free press from politicians with authoritarian motives and thin skins. In the 1720s when James Franklin printed in his newspaper, the *New England Courant*, that the Massachusetts government had not taken proper precautions against pirates, he was jailed for a month and a special legislative committee was appointed to deal with the matter. To avoid the consequences of a court order that his future publications be supervised, Franklin turned over publication of the newspaper to his younger brother, Benjamin. In another famous case, this in 1734, an indictment was drawn up by the Province of New York against John Peter Zenger for allegedly having printed a "certain false, malicious, seditious, libel, entitled the New York Weekly Journal". Zenger was more fortunate than James Franklin, as he won his case by turning it against the Government. Zenger argued that what he had printed was not libel but truth, and that it was the duty of free men to fight misrule and political corruption by disclosing the truth. Professor Bernard Rubin observes [217]: "Truth is not a gentle teacher. Often truth is cruel to the extreme, shoving and pushing the reluctant to change. Sometimes truth is the enemy of the powerful who are so fearful of change that they take up arms against armies of facts." Rubin reminds us that the Founding Fathers, in fashioning the Bill of Rights, were keenly aware of this history of travails of the American press.

Nonetheless, the courts must be careful to balance the rights of the plaintiff against those of the defendant in reaching a just settlement. Often the key element is whether the defendant can be shown to have malice towards the plaintiff—either outright hatred or negligence in not adequately documenting his "facts". Usually in the transmission of rumor there is no overt malice by the press, although one may be shown to be malicious for not having checked sources properly. In some states (particularly in New England), malice may even negate the defense of truth, if it can be proven that the malice was sufficiently intense.

Libel and slander laws have been generally effective in protecting the rights of private citizens. A more complicated issue concerns the rights of public officials and to what extent they should be protected from malicious or gossipy attacks. On 9 March 1974 the face of defamation law was greatly altered by the U.S. Supreme Court in its decision in the case of New York Times Co. versus Sullivan (376 U.S. 254, 1964).

In March of 1960, at the beginning of the Civil Rights movement in the South, a full page advertisement was placed in *The New York Times* by a group called "Committee to Defend Martin Luther King and the Struggle for Freedom in the South". The advertisement contained a series of charges against Alabama state officials. Five of the officials, including Montgomery Commissioner of Public Affairs L. B. Sullivan, felt that they had been libeled by the advertisement. Because the *Times* was distributed in Alabama, Sullivan was able to sue in his state court. It was shown during the course of the trial that a number of statements in the advertisement were inaccurate and that the *Times* had information in their news files to indicate that the advertisement did in fact contain false charges. The Alabama court found for Sullivan, awarded him $500,000, and the judgment was upheld in the Alabama Supreme Court. The *Times* then appealed to the United States Supreme Court, where they eventually won their historic reversal. The U.S. Supreme Court decision has given the press virtually an unrestricted license to criticize public officials, unless "actual malice" can be shown (that is, knowledge that the statement was false or with reckless disregard for its truth). In effect, the Court decided that the right of freedom of speech and of the press takes precedence in matters of public debate.

The Watergate affair and related scandals of the Nixon Administration have been heady for the American press. It seems nearly every young journalist seeks to emulate the example of the two *Washington Post* reporters, Woodward and Bernstein, who together uncovered much of the crucial information pertaining to Watergate. To some extent this is healthy, as politicians can no longer assume that their actions are immune to public scrutiny. However, due to this, a public official's private life must now be more circumspect.

The line between relevant information and titillating gossip is a thin one. The associate editor of the *Atlanta Constitution*, Hal Gulliver, has remarked [255, p. 84]: "The only rule of thumb I know is to consider how the public interest is involved." When does a politician's senility, drunkenness, lechery, or marital problems become a legitimate area for public scrutiny? Legally, there is little difficulty, morally the stakes are high. The key factor in the reporter's decision should be if the official's behavior affects the public performance of his duty. This rule is hard to apply. Brit Hume, a former associate of Jack Anderson, argues that the public is entitled to hear more about the private side of public figures than they are now being told [118]. But in their investigations the reporters should strive for a balanced viewpoint, rather than focusing on a single aspect of an official's life. Hume makes the important distinction between those who directly seek publicity (politicians, lecturers, advocates) and those who are brought into public life by others (the families of politicians). The latter are entitled to more privacy, he argues.

The press is not the only official group that collects gossip and rumor. Our own government gathers hearsay (as do some quasi-official agencies such as credit bureaus). Recent hearings by several congressional committees have uncovered there is an astoundingly large number of records on American citizens on file with this country's investigative agencies—some illegal. Many seem unrelated to any good purpose of national security or safety but are simply products of a bureaucracy gone out of control. Some have been used for unsavory purposes, such as discrediting a political enemy (as the F.B.I. did in the mid-1960s by leaking tapes of Martin Luther King Jr.'s extramarital sexual activities) [255]. We are now told that both John F. Kennedy and Lyndon B. Johnson were fond of reading the F.B.I.'s gossipy reports on their colleagues, which may be a reason the reports were collected in the first place.

One solution to this is to grant private citizens ready access to records about themselves with the right to sue the government and credit bureaus for misuse of such information. Congressional oversight of Federal agencies (the old alternative) has not proved a reliable safeguard for curbing the excesses of the F.B.I., C.I.A., or I.R.S. The goals and methods of curbing defamatory gossip and rumor will be different than those discussed in regard to combatting bogie and other malicious rumors of a more general nature. Here, time is not of the essence. Rather than invoke emergency measures, the rule of law must be allowed to take its course to protect individual dignity and social stability. However, in all cases, we need a sense of fairness, a dedication to the concepts of free speech and free press, and a sincere concern for public welfare and individual rights.

nine :: Conclusions

> Before embarking on a foreign assignment several
> years ago, a correspondent reporting on the State
> Department was called into the office of a high-
> ranking official who, without much ado, proceeded
> to "leak" a major story. On his way out, the news-
> man thanked the official but out of curiosity asked
> why he had been so honored.
>
> "Oh, I heard you were leaving and I thought it
> would be nice to give you a 'leak' for a going away
> present," the official replied.
>
> BERNARD GWERTZMAN
> *The New York Times*
> (March 14, 1976)

Substitute the dictionary definition of hearsay ("unverified,
unofficial information gained or acquired from another and not
part of one's direct knowledge") for the noun "leak" and the
Washington anecdote is succinctly indicative of the thesis of
this book. Passing rumors and gossip is an instrumental transaction in which A and B trade news for something in
return—more news, status, power, entertainment, money, social control, or any material or psychological stimulus capable
of fulfilling preconditioned needs, wishes, and expectations.
Gwertzman went on to remark: "Whatever the real motivation,
the official underscored a fact of Washington life: Information
is a valued commodity. It is handled by officials as other people might treat precious stones. It is admired, treasured, and
offered as a gift. Those who possess secrets are endowed with
the respect reserved for high priests in other societies."

Information, hearsay in particular, is indeed a valued commodity in the marketplace of social exchange, and its multiple functions and distribution patterns closely parallel the characteristics and rules of economic exchange. The consumption of rumor and gossip is analogous to the conspicuous consumption of goods and services, and it further attests to the wide generality of a habit which ignores most sociological and demographic boundaries. Moreover, this transactional nature is at odds with the classical definition portraying gossip as "idle chatter" as well as with the old stereotype which labels gossiping and rumormongering as feminine pursuits. There is ample evidence to refute both assertions: the phenomena are in essence purposive behaviors engaged in by everyone to varying degrees, whether consciously or by reflex, with distinct social and psychological functions attached to each.

We began this book with quoted definitions of rumor and gossip to show the circularity in common meaning of the concepts, one essentially being defined in terms of another. There is, of course, a type of hearsay which is indistinguishable as being distinctly rumor *or* gossip—the Paul McCartney tale is an example. However, most often the two can be readily distinguished. Rumor is thus characterized as unsubstantiated information on any issue or subject. Gossip is defined as small talk about personal affairs and people's activities with or without a known basis in fact; this definition goes somewhat beyond the common meaning of the generic term, hearsay.

Several typologies of rumor can identify the primary motivational bases, and perhaps the best one is Knapp's simple tripartite classification dividing rumors into pipe dreams (or wish rumors), bogies (fear or anxiety rumors), and wedge-drivers (aggression rumors). There are also three primary strains of gossip. Informative gossip exists for news trading and for providing participants with a cognitive map of the social environment. Moralising gossip is exploited as a manipulative device where one person attempts to gain an advantage over another. The third is engaged in strictly for mutual entertainment of the participants. However, the parallel between function and distribution is more clearly ordered in the case of gossip than of rumor. Informative gossip typically follows a redistributive trading pattern; the guiding principle is one of jus-

tice or fairness in accordance with individual or collective re-
quirements. Moralising gossip, said to function as a defensive
mechanism of the ego, conforms to a pattern of exchange
where the value of a commodity results from bargaining for
economic or psychological advantage. Gossiping for mutual entertainment is like reciprocative trade, which strives toward an
equitable ratio in the giving and receiving of goods and services.

In contrast to an earlier psychological model of rumor postulated by Allport and Postman, a more general model was constructed around experimental and correlational observations.
The transmission of both rumor and gossip was compared to
the transmission of information by a complex network of
neurons in the human nervous system. The energy used to excite the neuron is nonspecific, just as it appears to make little
difference in gossiping or rumormongering what kind of
energy is used to light the fuse. As long as the need-related
"excitation" is sufficiently strong, there will be ignition. There
is a different hierarchy of sources of intense energy between
rumor and gossip; the need for cognitive clarity being predominant for rumor and the need for status (or esteem) prevailing
for gossip. Stimulation of the neuron at the receptor is focused
onto the stem and then carried to minute nerve endings at
which point there is a gap where the excitation is transferred
to another neuron by chemical interaction. Chronic and acute
anxieties behave like the transmitter chemicals which aid in
the transfer of an excitation from one neuron to another. When
anxieties are concentrated, they should increase (up to a point)
the efficiency of rumor and gossip transmissions. Hence, with
rumor, ambiguity is the prepotent energy used to excite, anxiety is the transmitter chemical which speeds information on its
way.

More than 40 years ago Kirkpatrick called for systematic research into the psychology of rumor, and as evidenced by the
variety of literature cited here, it is clear that his message
drew a wide response. However, while much of a preliminary
empirical nature is known, unanswered questions about personality correlates and situational conditions in the origin and
transmission of rumor and gossip still exist awaiting careful

scientific exploration and verification. The marketplace and biological metaphors are advanced here as alternative hypotheses to serve as conceptual embarkation points for further theoretical and empirical inquiry.

appendix : : Standards and Guidelines for Rumor Control Centers

The Community Relations Service of the U.S. Department of Justice arranged a conference in Chicago in 1968 on the subject of "The Value of Establishing Rumor Control Centers." Participating were more than a hundred directors and representatives of various local and regional organizations throughout the country associated with rumor control. In 1974 a synthesis of the conference proceedings and other data was developed by Arthur A. Peltz for the Community Relations Service as an in-house report under the title "Purpose and Usefulness of Rumor Control or Verification Center." The following is an edited and slightly abridged version of the Peltz memorandum, previously unpublished.

Rumor is defined as information of an indiscernible nature. The *Report of the National Advisory Commission on Civil Disorders* concluded:

Rumors significantly aggravated tension and disorder in more than 65 percent of the disorders studied by the Commission. Sometimes, as in Tampa and New Haven, rumor served as the spark which turned an incident into a civil disorder. Elsewhere, notably Detroit and Newark, even where they were not precipitating or motivating factors, inflaming rumors made the job of police and community leaders far more difficult. Experience also has shown that the harmful effect of rumors can be offset if police, public officials, and community leaders quickly and effectively circulate the facts .... An innovative method is that of a 'Rumor Central'—an office responsible for the collection, evaluation, and countering of rumors which could lead to civil disorder.

The harmful effects of rumors can be offset by establishing a communication system to verify and disseminate reliable information. Prior to its establishment, however, it is necessary to define the purpose for the establishment of the verification center. An effective center can be an ad hoc service operational only during periods of crisis, or it can operate as a full-time service to meet community needs for emergency information (i.e., an information or counseling hot line to deal with threatened suicides, runaways, drug abuses, consumer information, environmental complaints). Centers should be a service, not merely a pacifier.

AUSPICES

A center can only be effective if it operates with the sanction of municipal authority's highest office (the mayor, the city manager). In addition to the cooperation and endorsement of community leaders, one can enlist a human relations commission to be the responsible agency for supervising a center. The National Advisory Commission noted: "To be most effective, such units might be located outside police departments. In any event, they should work closely with police and other officials." Historically, local law enforcement agencies are concerned with quick containment of disorder, not with rumors about present or future trouble. Therefore, it is suggested that the center be operated outside those agencies.

BUDGETING

In developing a budget to make a feasible funding request it is well to keep in mind that if the amount requested is insufficient, and an emergency arises requiring immediate funds, the normal procurement procedures might not respond fast enough. This could result in a slipshod operation from the outset. Conversely, if the amount requested is too high, it might be rejected out of hand.

The largest single expense will probably be staff salaries. To minimize costs (and for other reasons to be discussed subsequently), the use of volunteers is encouraged.

Telephone installation and operation constitute another major expense. A rumor control center in Denver, Colorado utilized municipal phones through the cooperation of the mayor's office. A center in Oklahoma City was able to have telephones installed at the rate quoted for all city official telephones. Chicago absorbed the cost of phones as normal city operating costs, while Detroit had the city Human Relations Commission absorb costs. The mayor of Baton Rouge used contingency funds for installation and service; however, both the professional and volunteer staff were reimbursed by the local CAP agency. In Jackson, Mississippi the state university approved the operation and maintenance of the center as a university project under the direction of the psychology department; students received grade credit for work at the center.

In developing an approximate budget, it is advisable to include the following items:

A supervisory staff member (full-time)
Two telephone lines for use by verifiers
Three to six incoming phones on a rotary, with light buttons
    if possible
An office large enough to accommodate three to six operators
A small adjoining office for verifier (desirable, but not mandatory), pads, pencils, tables, chairs, blackboards, utilities, snacks, and beverages for crews.

As a rough indicator of the salary level for the center supervisory person, Dayton, Ohio contracted someone to provide services for 16 weeks for the sum of $1,440. All personnel except supervisory are required to answer and verify calls during grave emergency when volume is high. At such times the center is manned on a 24-hour basis. The day shift could be from 8 a.m. to 7 p.m.; the night shift, from 7 p.m. to 8 a.m. When the volume of calls diminishes, the center can operate on a 12-hour basis, from 8 a.m. to 8 p.m.

Earlier, reference was made to other types of information that might be requested from a verification center. In Washington, D.C., the center reported the following:

Handled 1500 calls per 24-hour period
Maintained constant contact with police, fire, media, and other vital community services
Funneled donations of food, clothing, shelter, and money to appropriate sources in the community
Attained through volunteers thousands of dollars of donated food and medical and baby supplies
Provided individuals personalized emergency care for families in crisis with such things as delivery of clothing, food and furniture
Emergency transportation for displaced families; emergency medical assistance
Provided emergency temporary housing services; assisted in establishing housing relocation center.

In this context, the center could function on a year-round basis in cooperation with traditional community services.

OPERATION

The center must be responsive to situational needs that arise. During periods of routine activity it can function as an information center, thereby enabling citizens to become accustomed to using it as a reliable and credible referral source. In this way, when an emergency arises, citizens will turn to the center for information, through habit, as they have been accustomed to doing during noncritical times. Cities which, as of 1974, operated full-time centers were Chicago, Denver, Detroit, Lansing, Miami, and Boston. In noncritical times the operations are geared to preparation for emergencies by giving staff members and volunteers experience in handling inquiries and using referral services. In times of crisis, these centers quickly shift into high gear. The standby telephone can be hooked up, and it is possible to activate rumor verification at peak effectiveness in a short time.

Operators should be trained to handle incoming calls in a calm, professional manner. Basic instructions should include (but not be limited to) the following rules:

1. Avoid philosophical discussions and arguments.
2. Don't give callers a complete rundown on what is happening in the city. Urge callers to check local radio, television, or newspapers.
3. Don't spread rumors—use common sense.
4. Don't prolong or encourage lengthy conversations.
5. Don't volunteer information.
6. Don't lie or mislead callers.
7. Discourage giving personal identification or location of the center in times of crisis.
8. Don't ridicule or admonish callers.

This list can be expanded as experience dictates. Supervisors or verifiers are used to contact specific check-points for verification of rumors. These check-points include the police, fire officials, hospitals, the media, the mayor's office, as well as other previously arranged sources of accurate information. Only verified information is given to operators.

A good center remains flexible and adaptive to whatever changes occur should the particulars of a situation shift. In times of crisis many callers want to know "What's the latest rumor?" Remember, the center is there to dispel, not to propel rumors.

VERIFICATION GUIDELINES

The ability to establish credibility within a community as well as with various agencies will determine the success or failure of a center. This credibility is established and enhanced by a careful selection of sources chosen to verify the information requiring confirmation. The procedure for verification should be meticulous and methodical so that no inaccuracies are disseminated. For this reason authorization to cooperate and disseminate information must be mandated by the highest levels of government (municipal, state, county).

The following is a partial list of contact-points that can be included in the directory of resources used for verification of specific information.

The Governor's Office

Mayor's Office

County Executive Office

Police Chief and/or State Highway Police

Fire Chief/Office of Public Safety

Office of Public Services/Office of Emergency Preparedness

Superintendent of Schools/Public/Parochial/College

National Guard/Reserves

Hospital: Public Information Office

Radio/TV/Newspapers/Publishers (Minority Press and Soul Station)

All Transportation Depots/Airports/Railways/Buses

Local Community Organizations: NAACP, IMAGE, League of Women Voters, Urban League

Chamber of Commerce/Jay Cee/AIM/CAP/United Way.

Local conditions and facilities will dictate additional contacts, such as the public information office of a large corporation. This is especially helpful should the community be a "company town."

The center should designate individuals who are identified as verifiers to their counterparts in the contact-points listed above. An understanding should be reached that there be a free and rapid flow of information whenever an inquiry is made by authorized verifiers. On-site contacts preferably should be employees or representatives who are thoroughly familiar with their respective organizations and capable of an immediate decision as to the extent of information provided to verifiers. For purposes of control and confidentiality, authorized verifiers should be kept to a minimum.

Verifiers through training and experience should learn to evaluate, digest, and transmit information to telephone operators in a manner that will not excite or exaggerate conditions. Verifiers should be responsible for producing a daily fact sheet (or update report) that can be made available to the media for public dissemination.

Centers serving communities with as few as 50,000 population ranging to as many as 100,000 have functioned with two verifiers. An increase in personnel may be called for if community tensions increase, if the volume of calls per hour drastically increases, or if it becomes difficult to reach contact-points. In those centers where limited personnel are available, it may be necessary to combine the responsibilities of verifiers and coordinators.

To function effectively there must be good rapport between verifiers and operators. Using volunteers may increase the likelihood of finding personnel who are highly motivated and conscientious. The tenor of operations is often reflected by this attitude; tension and apprehension can be easily detected. Callers are quick to sense this atmosphere and to misinterpret its real cause. Maintaining a calm demeanor in situations that by their nature excite, should be uppermost in the minds of all personnel. It also helps to have sufficient working space so that personnel aren't literally bumping into one another.

In summary, let it be understood that a verifier is likened to a commanding officer. The decision making process begins and ends at his or her desk.

OPERATORS

As voice contact is the primary link between community and information sources, it is the most sensitive and critical facet of a center. It is not uncommon even for a sophisticated system to be ineffective or counterproductive because an operator was chosen without appropriate consideration. He or she should have the following qualities:

1. Ability to be understood quickly
2. Ability to vocally project a calm, confident demeanor
3. Ability to deal with local slang, foreign dialects and language, and a variety of linguistic styles
4. Familiarity with the geography of the community
5. Ability to terminate nonproductive, obscene, or threatening calls
6. Ability to prolong a call should it become necessary
7. Ability to respond patiently without becoming emotionally aroused by a caller's excitement.

When an operator becomes fatigued or hungry, or if his/her emotional energies are spent, efficiency declines. An alert coordinator periodically monitors the operators to insure continuity of performance level. The voice the public hears can make or break an operation. Review carefully the foregoing suggestions and be sure to incorporate them in the training of operators.

A mechanical device such as a code-a-phone can be used to serve in off-peak hours, provided the messages are then cleared at reasonable intervals. Instances sometimes occur when a caller becomes resentful talking to a machine. However, handled prudently on an "as needed" basis, the mechanical message receiver can be a valuable adjunct to a system.

Another duty of an operator is to log every call, noting time, type, and whether a call-back is required. Terminating every call with a polite "thank you for calling" goes a long way in maintaining public trust and community support. Volunteer operators should be expected to deliver the same performance level that a paid or professional operator provides.

MEDIA RELATIONS

The term media here refers to all channels of news reporting, including weekly newspapers, the minority press, ethnic and foreign language radio stations, educational and independent television. The use of the media is critical in publicizing the center's role in the community—by familiarizing the public with its aims and goals as well as its hours of operation and, of course, telephone number. While it is appropriate for the center to compile and to circulate a fact sheet for the press, the press should be discouraged from using the center as a principal source for community news. The press should not publicize the center's location during a crisis situation. Publicizing a center's telephone number and urging the public to call, however, will avoid having the media unnecessarily burdened with inquiries. A balanced working relationship should be established at the outset: centers and the media perform their own functions in a mutually beneficial way. Press facilities have, on certain occasions, been provided close to a center—not for the purpose of observing the center and its activities, but to be close to a spokesman or official who is authorized to issue statements regarding a crisis situation. For example, the Washington, D.C. Command Center maintained adjacent press facilities since the city's mayor directed and monitored crises from that location. The actual operations room, however, was "off limits to working press during crises." Press should be kept advised of center hours, and it would be helpful if the media frequently publicized these hours as a public service. It can also be helpful to keep a flow or exchange of information.

RESOURCES

While no two communities are identical, many do share common resources that can be tapped either for volunteer personnel or for funding. The following partial list may be helpful in these areas. Ingenuity, research, and knowledge of your community will add to your own list of possibilities.

FUNDING

Federal Sources
  HEW/Emergency Medical Services of October 1973
  LEAA/Discretionary grants to improve communications
  OEA/Office of Emergency Assistance

State
  Office of Emergency Preparedness
  Governor's Office (emergency funds)
Local
  Mayor's Office (emergency funds)
  County Executives (emergency funds)
  Office of Civil Preparedness

References

1. Adams, J. S. "Inequity in social exchange." *Advances in Experimental Social Psychology*, edited by L. Berkowitz, vol. 2. New York: Academic Press, 1965.
2. Adams, J. T. "Our whispering campaigns." *Harper's Monthly Magazine* 165(1932): 444–50.
3. Addams, J. "A modern devil-baby." *American Journal of Sociology* 20(1914): 117–18.
4. Adorno, T. W.; Frenkel-Brunswik, E.; Levinson, D. J.; and Sanford, R. N. *The Authoritarian Personality*. New York: Harper, 1950.
5. Allport, F. H., and Lepkin, M. "Wartime rumors of waste and special privilege: why some people believe them." *Journal of Abnormal and Social Psychology* 40(1945): 3–36.
6. Allport, G. W. *The Nature of Prejudice*. New York: Doubleday Anchor, 1954.
7. Allport, G. W., and Faden, J. M. "The psychology of newspapers: five tentative laws." *Public Opinion Quarterly* 4(1940): 678–703.
8. Allport, G. W., and Postman, L. J. "The basic psychology of

rumor." *New York Academy of Sciences Transactions* 8(1945): 61–81.

9. Allport, G. W., and Postman, L. J. "An analysis of rumor." *Public Opinion Quarterly* 10(1947): 501–517.

10. Allport, G. W., and Postman, L. J. *The Psychology of Rumor.* New York: Holt, Rinehart & Winston, 1947.

11. Angoff, C. *The Book of Libel.* New York: A. S. Barnes, 1966.

12. Anthony, S. "Anxiety and rumor." *Journal of Social Psychology* 89(1973): 91–98.

13. Ashley, P.P. *Say It Safely: Legal Limits in Publishing, Radio, and Television.* 3rd ed. Seattle: University of Washington Press, 1966.

14. Atwood, L. E. "How newsmen and readers perceive each others' story preferences." *Journalism Quarterly* 47(1970): 296–303.

15. Atwood, L. E., and Grotta, G. L. "Socialization of news values in beginning reporters." *Journalism Quarterly* 50(1973): 759–61.

16. Back, K.; Festinger, L. Hymovitch, B.; Kelley, H.; Schachter, S.; and Thibaut, J. "The methodology of studying rumor transmission." *Human Relations,* 3(1950): 307–12.

17. Barth, F. "Economic spheres in Darfur." *Themes in Economic Anthropology,* edited by R. Firth. London: Tavistock, 1967.

18. Bartlett, F. C. *Remembering: A Study in Experimental and Social Psychology.* Cambridge: Cambridge University Press, 1932.

19. Bauer, R. A., and Gleicher, D. B. "Word-of-mouth communication in the Soviet Union." *Public Opinion Quarterly* 17(1953): 297–310.

20. Belgion, M. "The vogue of rumor." *Quarterly Review* 273(1939): 1–18.

21. Bey, A. S. A. R. "Rumor." *Egyptian Journal of Psychology* 5(1949): 2–18. (English summary)

22. Biberian, M. J.; Anthony, S.; and Rosnow, R. L. "Some determining factors in the transmission of a rumor." Unpublished study, London School of Economics and Temple University, 1975.

23. Blake, R. H. "The relationship between collective excitement and rumor construction." *Rocky Mountain Social Science Journal* 6(1969): 119–126.

24. Blau, P. *Exchange and Power in Social Life.* New York: Wiley, 1964.

25. Blum, J. M. "Tumulty and Leavenworth: a case study of rumor." *Journal of Abnormal and Social Psychology* 44(1949): 411–13.

26. Blumenthal, A. "The nature of gossip." *Sociology and Social Research* 22(1937): 31–37.

27. Bogart, L. "The spread of news on a local event: a case history." *Public Opinion Quarterly* 14(1950): 769–72.

28. Bowers, D. R. "A report on activity by publishers in directing newsroom decisions." *Journalism Quarterly* 44(1967): 43–52.

29. Breed, W. "Social control in the newsroom: a functional analysis." *Social Forces* 33(1955): 326–35.

30. Brissey, F. L. "The factor of relevance in the serial transmission of information." *Journal of Communication* 11(1961): 211–19.
31. Britt, G. *Rumors (Made in Germany)*. New York: Council for Democracy—National Committee on the Cause and Cure of War, 1942.
32. Brock, T. C. "Implications of commodity theory for value change." *Psychological Foundations of Attitudes*, edited by A. G. Greenwald; T. C. Brock; and T. M. Ostrom. New York: Academic Press, 1968.
33. Buckhout, R. "Eyewitness testimony." *Scientific American* 231, no. 6(1974): 23–31.
34. Buckner, H. T. "A theory of rumor transmission." *Public Opinion Quarterly* 29(1965): 54–70.
35. Butler, S. D. "Dame rumor: the biggest liar in the world." *American Magazine* 111(1931): 24–26, 155–56.
36. Campbell, D. T. "Systematic error on the part of human links in communication systems." *Information and Control* 1(1958): 334–69.
37. Cantril, H. *The Invasion From Mars*. Princeton: Princeton University Press, 1940.
38. Caplow, T. "Rumors in war." *Social Forces* 25(1947): 298–302.
39. Carter-Ruck, P. F. *Libel & Slander*. London: Faber & Faber, 1972.
40. Champion, F. R.; Taylor, R.; Joseph, P. R.; and Hedden, J. C. "Mass hysteria associated with insect bites." *Journal of the South Carolina Medical Association* 59(1963): 351–53.
41. Chaudhuri, P. "A synopsis of an experimental attempt on the study of psychology of rumor." *Indian Journal of Psychology* 28(1953): 79–86.
42. Chorus, A. "The basic law of rumor." *Journal of Abnormal and Social Psychology* 48(1953): 313–14.
43. Clevenger, T., Jr., and Knepprath, E. "A quantitative analysis of logical and emotional content in selected campaign addresses of Eisenhower and Stevenson." *Western Speech* Summer(1966): 144–50.
44. Clyde, R. W., and Buckalew, R. "Inter-media standardization: a Q-analysis of news editors." *Journalism Quarterly* 46(1969): 349–51.
45. Cohen, D. *A Modern Look at Monsters*. New York: Dodd, Mead, 1970.
46. Coleman, J. S. *The Mathematics of Collective Action*. Chicago: Aldine, 1973.
47. Colson, E. *The Makah Indians*. Manchester, England: Manchester University Press, 1953. Also published by University of Minnesota Press.
48. Cook, T. D.; Gruder, C. L.; Hennigan, K. M.; and Halamaj, J. "The sleeper effect in the context of the discounting cue hypothesis." Unpublished paper, Northwestern University, 1975.
49. Cooley, C. H. *Social Organization*. New York: Schocken Books,

1962. Originally published 1909.

50. Corrozi, J. F., and Rosnow, R. L. "Consonant and dissonant communications as positive and negative reinforcements in opinion change." *Journal of Personality and Social Psychology* 8(1968): 27–30.

51. Cox, B. "What is Hopi gossip about? information management and Hopi factions." *Man* 5(1970): 88–98.

52. Crawshaw, R. "Gossip wears a thousand masks." *Prism* 2(1974): 45–47.

53. Crittenden, J. "Democratic function of the open-mike radio forum." *Public Opinion Quarterly* 35(1971): 200–210.

54. Danzig, E. R.; Galanter, P. W.; and Galanter, L. R. *The Effects of a Threatening Rumor on a Disaster-Stricken Community.* Washington, D.C.: National Academy of Sciences—National Research Council, 1958. Publication 517.

55. Davis, K. "Management communication and the grapevine." *Harvard Business Review* 31(1953): 43–49.

56. Davis, K. "Grapevine communication among lower and middle managers." *Personnel Journal* 48(1969): 269–72.

57. Davis, K. *Human Behavior at Work: Human Relations and Organization Behavior.* 4th ed. New York: McGraw-Hill, 1972.

58. DeFleur, M. L., and Larsen, O. N. *The Flow of Information.* New York: Harper, 1958.

59. Degh, L., and Vazsonyi, A. "The hypothesis of multi-conduit transmission in folklore." *Folklore, Communication, and Performance*, edited by D. Ben-Amos and K. Goldstein. The Hague, Netherlands: Mouton Press, 1974.

60. Deutscher, I., and New, P. K-M. "A functional analysis of collective behavior in a disaster." *Sociological Quarterly* 2(1961): 21–36.

61. Dodd, S. C. "A test of message diffusion by chain tags." *American Journal of Sociology* 61(1956): 425–32.

62. Dodd, S. C. "Formulas for spreading opinions." *Public Opinion Quarterly* 22(1958): 537–54.

63. Dollard, J., and Miller, N. E. *Personality and Psychotherapy.* New York: McGraw-Hill, 1950.

64. Donohew, L. "Newspaper gatekeepers and forces in the news channel." *Public Opinion Quarterly* 31(1967): 61–68.

65. Drabek, T. E., and Stephenson, J. S., III. "When disaster strikes." *Journal of Applied Social Psychology* 1(1971): 187–203.

66. Durkheim, E. *Suicide.* Translated by J. A. Spaulding and G. Simpson. Glencoe, Illinois: Free Press, 1951.

67. Eells, G. *Hedda and Louella.* New York: Warner, 1972.

68. Efron, E. *The News Twisters.* Los Angeles: Nash, 1971.

69. Epstein, E. J. *News From Nowhere: Television and the News.* New York: Random House, 1973.

70. Fathi, A. "Diffusion of a 'happy' news event." *Journalism Quarterly* 50(1973): 271–77.

71. Fathi, A. "Problems in developing indices of news value." *Journalism Quarterly* 50(1973): 497–501.

72. Festinger, L. "A theory of social comparison." *Human Relations* 7(1954): 117–40.
73. Festinger, L. *A Theory of Cognitive Dissonance.* Evanston, Illinois: Row, Peterson, 1957.
74. Festinger, L.; Cartwright, D.; Barber, K.; Fleischl, J.; Gottsdanker, J.; Keysen, A.; and Leavitt, G. "A study of rumor: its origin and spread." *Human Relations* 1(1948): 464–85.
75. Festinger, L.; Schachter, S.; and Back, K. *Social Pressures of Informal Groups.* New York: Harper, 1950.
76. Fine, G. A. "The diffusion and recall of information: news in the aftermath of the Agnew resignation." *Journalism Quarterly,* in press.
77. Firth, R. "Rumor in a primitive society." *Journal of Abnormal and Social Psychology* 53(1956): 122–32.
78. Foa, U. G. "Interpersonal and economic resources." *Science* 171(1971): 345–51.
79. Foa, U. G., and Foa, E. B. *Societal Structures of the Mind.* Chicago: Chas. Thomas, 1974.
80. Frank, R. S. *Message Dimensions of Television News.* Lexington, Mass.: D. C. Heath, 1973.
81. Frenkel-Brunswik, E. "Intolerance of ambiguity as an emotional and perceptual variable." *Journal of Personality* 18(1949): 108–43.
82. Frenkel-Brunswik, E. "Personality theory and perception." *Perception: An Approach to Personality,* edited by R. R. Blake and G. V. Ramsey. New York: Ronald, 1951.
83. Freud, S. "The psychopathology of everyday life." *The Standard Edition of the Complete Psychological Works of Sigmund Freud,* edited and translated by J. Strachey, vol. 6. London: Hogarth Press, 1960.
84. Fromkin, H. L.; Olson, J. C.; Dipboye, R. L.; and Barnaby, D. A. "A commodity theory analysis of consumer preferences for scarce products." *Proceedings of the 79th Annual Convention of the American Psychological Association* 6(1971): 653–54.
85. Garfinkel, H. "Conditions of successful degradation ceremonies." *American Journal of Sociology* 61(1956): 420–24.
86. Garfinkel, H. *Studies in Ethnomethodology.* Englewood Cliffs: Prentice-Hall, 1967.
87. Gaston, J. "Secretiveness and competition for priority of discovery in physics." *Minerva* 9(1971): 472–92.
88. Gergen, K. *The Psychology of Behavior Exchange.* Reading, Mass.: Addison-Wesley, 1969.
89. Gieber, W. "How the 'gatekeepers' view local civil liberties news." *Journalism Quarterly* 37(1960): 199–206.
90. Giffin, K. "The contribution of studies of source credibility to a theory of interpersonal trust in the communication process." *Psychological Bulletin* 68(1967): 104–20.
91. Gillig, P. M., and Greenwald, A. G. "Is it time to lay the sleeper effect to rest?" *Journal of Personality and Social Psychology* 29(1974): 132–39.

92. Gluckman, M. "Gossip and scandal." *Current Anthropology* 4(1963): 307-16.
93. Godwin, W. F., and Restle, F. "The road to agreement: subgroup pressures in small group consensus processes." *Journal of Personality and Social Psychology* 30(1974): 500-509.
94. Goffman, E. *Stigma.* Englewood Cliffs: Prentice-Hall, 1963.
95. Goffman, E. *Strategic Interaction.* Philadelphia: University of Pennsylvania Press, 1969.
96. Gold, D., and Simmons, J. L. "News selection patterns among Iowa dailies." *Public Opinion Quarterly* 29(1965): 425-36.
97. Goldhaber, S. Z. "Medical education: Harvard reverts to tradition." *Science* 181(1973): 1027-32.
98. Goldstein, J. H. *Aggression and Crimes of Violence.* New York: Oxford, 1975.
99. Greenberg, B. S. "Diffusion of news of the Kennedy assassination." *Public Opinion Quarterly* 28(1964): 225-32.
100. Hall, M. "The great cabbage hoax: a case study." *Journal of Personality and Social Psychology* 2(1965): 563-69.
101. Hall, S. "External-internal dialectic in broadcasting: television's double-bind." *Fourth Symposium on Broadcasting Policy,* edited by F. S. Bradley. Manchester, England: University of Manchester Department of Extra-Mural Studies, 1972.
102. Hannerz, U. "Gossip, networks and culture in a black American ghetto." *Ethnos* 32(1967): 35-60.
103. Harris, M. "Conspiracy to the left of us! paranoia to the right of us!" *The New York Times Magazine,* August 24, 1975, pp. 12, 49-50, 54.
104. Hart, B. "The psychology of rumor." *Proceedings of the Royal Society of Medicine (Section on Psychiatry),* March, 1916.
105. Haviland, J. B. "Gossip, gossips, and gossiping in Zinacaritan." Doctoral dissertation, Harvard University Department of Social Relations, 1971.
106. Heisenberg, W. *Across the Frontiers.* Translated by P. Heath. New York: Harper & Row, 1974.
107. Henderson, E. H. "A study of memory." *Psychological Monographs* 5, no. 23(1903).
108. Hershey, R. "Heed rumors for their meaning." *Personnel Journal* 34(1956): 299-301.
109. Herskovits, M. *Life in a Haitian Valley.* New York: Knopf, 1937.
110. Higham, T.M. "The experimental study of the transmission of rumor." *British Journal of Psychology* 42(1951): 42-55.
111. Hill, R. J., and Bonjean, C. M. "News diffusion: a test of the regularity hypothesis." *Journalism Quarterly* 41(1964): 336-42.
112. Holton, G. *Thematic Origins of Scientific Thought: Kepler to Einstein.* Cambridge, Mass.: Harvard, 1973.
113. Holton, G. "On the role of themata in scientific thought." *Science* 188(1975): 328-34.
114. Homans, G. C. "Social behavior as exchange." *American Journal of Sociology* 63(1958): 597-606.

115. Homans, G. C. *Social Behavior: Its Elementary Forms.* rev. ed. New York: Harcourt-Brace-Jovanovich, 1974.

116. Hovland, C. I., and Weiss, W. "The influence of source credibility on communication effectiveness." *Public Opinion Quarterly* 15(1951): 635–50.

117. Hufford, R. A. "The place of ambiguity in political speaking." Doctoral dissertation, Southern Illinois University, 1962. University Microfilms 62–1568.

118. Hume, B. "The private lives of public people." *Boston Sunday Globe,* April 27, 1975, p. B3.

119. Irvin, E. J. "Corpus delicti." *Collective Behavior,* edited by R. H. Turner and L. M. Killian. Englewood Cliffs: Prentice-Hall, 1957.

120. Irving, J. A. "The psychological analysis of wartime rumor patterns in Canada." *Bulletin of the Canadian Psychological Association* 3(1943): 40–44.

121. Jacobs, J. *The Death and Life of Great American Cities.* New York: Random House, 1961.

122. Jacobson, D. J. *The Affairs of Dame Rumor.* New York: Rinehart, 1948.

123. Jenkins, J. J. "Remember that old theory of memory? well, forget it!" *American Psychologist* 29(1974): 785–95.

124. Johnson, D. M. "The 'phantom anesthetist' of Mattoon: a field study of mass hysteria." *Journal of Abnormal and Social Psychology* 40(1945): 175–86.

125. Jourard, S. M. *Self-Disclosure: An Experimental Analysis of the Transparent Self.* New York: Wiley-Interscience, 1971.

126. Jung, C. G. "Ein Beitrag zur Psychologie des Gerüchtes." *Zentralblatt für Psychoanalyse* 1(1910): 81–90.

127. Jung, C. G. "A contribution to the psychology of rumor." *Collected Papers on Analytic Psychology.* 2nd ed. London: Barlliere, Tindall & Cox, 1922.

128. Jung, C. G. "A visionary rumor." *Journal of Analytical Psychology* 4(1959): 5–19.

129. Kaats, G. R., and Davis, K. E. "The social psychology of sexual behavior." *Social Psychology in the Seventies,* edited by L. S. Wrightsman. Monterey, California: Brooks/Cole, 1972.

130. Katona, G. "The relationship between psychology and economics." *Psychology: A Study of a Science,* edited by S. Koch, vol. 6. New York: McGraw-Hill, 1963.

131. Katz, D., and Stotland, E. "A preliminary statement to a theory of attitude structure and change." *Psychology: A Study of a Science,* edited by S. Koch, vol. 3. New York: McGraw-Hill, 1959.

132. Katz, E., and Lazarsfeld, P. F. *Personal Influence: The Part Played by People in the Flow of Mass Communications.* New York: Free Press, 1955.

133. Kelman, H. C., and Hovland, C. I. " 'Reinstatement' of the communicator in delayed measurement of opinion change." *Journal of Abnormal and Social Psychology* 48(1953): 327–35.

134. Kerckhoff, A., and Back, K. *The June Bug: A Study of Hysterical Contagion*. New York: Appleton-Century-Crofts, 1968.
135. Kerchoff, A., C.; Back, K. W.; and Miller, N. "Sociometric patterns in hysterial contagion." *Sociometry* 28(1965): 2–15.
136. Kerner. O., et al. *Report of the National Advisory Commission on Civil Disorders*. New York: Bantam, 1968.
137. Kirkpatrick, C. "A tentative study in experimental social psychology." *American Journal of Sociology* 28(1932): 194–206.
138. Kishler, J. P.; Yarnold, K. W.; Daly, J. M.; McCabe, F. I.; and Orlansky, J. "The use of rumor in psychological warfare." *A Psychological Warfare Casebook*, edited by W. E. Daugherty and M. Janowitz. Baltimore: Johns Hopkins Press, 1960.
139. Knapp, R. H. "A psychology of rumor." *Public Opinion Quarterly* 8(1944): 22–37.
140. Knight, J. A.; Friedman, T. I.; and Sulitani, J. "Epidemic hysteria: a field study." *American Journal of Public Health* 55(1965): 858–65.
141. Knopf, T. A. *Rumors, Race and Riots*. New Brunswick, New Jersey: Transaction Books, 1975.
142. Knopf, T. A. "Rumor controls: a reappraisal." *Phylon* 36, no. 1(1975): 23–31.
143. Lana, R. E., and Rosnow, R. L. *Introduction to Contemporary Psychology*. New York: Holt, Rinehart & Winston, 1972.
144. Lang, K., & Lang, G. *Collective Dynamics*. New York: Crowell, 1961.
145. Larsen, O. N. "Rumors in a disaster." *Journal of Communication* 4(1954): 111–23.
146. Larsen, O. N., and Hill, R. J. "Mass media and interpersonal communication in the diffusion of a news event." *American Sociological Review* 19(1954): 426–33.
147. Lawrence, G. C., and Grey, D. L. "Subjective inaccuracies in local news reporting." *Journalism Quarterly* 46(1969): 753–57.
148. Layton, C. "The great pearl discovery was just a whim." *Philadelphia Inquirer*, July 14, 1974, p. 6B.
149. Lazarsfeld, P. F.; Berelson, B.; and Gaudet, H. *The People's Choice*. New York: Duell, Sloan & Pearce, 1944.
150. Lefever, E. W. *TV and National Defense: An Analysis of CBS News, 1972–1973*. Boston, Virginia: Institute for American Strategy, 1974.
151. Le Gallienne, R. "The psychology of gossip." *Munsey's Magazine* 48(1912): 123–27.
152. Lewin, K. "Frontiers in group dynamics: II. channels of group life: social planning and action research." *Human Relations* 1(1947): 143–53.
153. Li, R. P. Y., and Thompson, W. R. "The 'coup contagion' hypothesis." *Journal of Conflict Resolution* 19, no. 1(1975): 63–88.
154. Loewenberg, R. D. "Rumors of mass poisoning in times of crisis." *Journal of Criminal Psychopathology* 5(1943): 131–42.

155. Logan, J. D. "The psychology of gossip." *Canadian Magazine* 31(1908): 106–11.

156. Longabaugh, R. "A category system for coding interpersonal behavior as social exchange." *Sociometry* 26(1963): 319–44.

157. Lowe, H. "The psychology of rumour." *The Medical Press and Circular* 206(1941): 219–21.

158. Lumley, F. E. *Means of Social Control.* New York: The Century Co., 1925.

159. Mailer, N. *Marilyn: A Biography.* New York: Grosset & Dunlap, 1973.

160. Manis, M.; Cornell, S. D.; and Moore, J. C. "Transmission of attitude-relevant information through a communication chain." *Journal of Personality and Social Psychology* 30(1974): 81–94.

161. Mausner, J. S., and Gezon, H. M. "Report on a phantom epidemic of gonorrhea." *American Journal of Epidemiology* 85(1967): 320–31.

162. McCormick, E. "Boston's fight against rumors." *American Mercury* 55(1942): 275–81.

163. McGinnies, E. *Social Behavior: A Functional Analysis.* Boston: Houghton Mifflin, 1970.

164. McGinnis, H. C. "Rumor." *Catholic Digest* 6(1942): 94–97.

165. McGuire, W. J. "Inducing resistance to persuasion: some contemporary approaches." *Advances in Experimental Social Psychology,* edited by L. Berkowitz, vol. 1, New York: Academic Press, 1964.

166. Medalia, N. Z., and Larsen, O. N. "Diffusion and belief in a collective delusion: the Seattle windshield pitting epidemic." *American Sociological Review* 23(1958): 180–86.

167. Mencken, H. L. *The American Language.* 4th ed. New York: Knopf, 1962.

168. Mendelsohn, H. "Behaviorism, functionalism, and mass communications policy." *Public Opinion Quarterly* 38(1974): 379–89.

169. Merton, R. K. "Self-fulfilling prophecy." *Antioch Review* 8(1948): 193–210.

170. Merton, R. K. "Thematic analysis in science: notes on Holton's concept." *Science* 188(1975): 335–38.

171. Mes, G. M. "It is natural to obey." *The Mankind Quarterly* 15(1975): 211–21.

172. Middleton, J., and Runner, P. M. "Community information center." *Journal of Intergroup Relations* 1(1972): 3–39.

173. Milgram, S. "The small-world problem." *Readings in Social Psychology Today,* edited by J. V. McConnell. Del Mar, California: CRM Books, 1970.

174. Milgram, S., and Toch, H. "Collective behavior: crowds and social movements." *The Handbook of Social Psychology,* edited by G. Lindzey and E. Aronson. 2nd ed., vol. 4. Reading, Massachusetts: Addison-Wesley, 1969.

175. Morgan, E. P. "Washington's no. 1 hostess: dame rumor." *The New York Times Magazine,* February 11, 1962, pp. 29, 39, 40, 42.

176. Morin, E. *Rumor in Orléans*. Translated by P. Green. New York: Pantheon, 1971.
177. Moynihan, M. "The great Nazi chunnel scare." *The Sunday Times* (London), July 15, 1973.
178. Naughton, J. M. "How the 2nd best-informed man in the White House briefs the 2nd worst-informed group in Washington." *The New York Times Magazine*, May 30, 1971, pp. 21, 24–27, 30.
179. Nichols, L. L. "A crowd observation." *Collective Behavior*, edited by R. H. Turner and L. M. Killian. Englewood Cliffs: Prentice-Hall, 1957.
180. Niehoff, A. H. *Intra-Group Communication and Induced Change*. Washington, D. C.: Human Resources Research Office. No. 25–67.
181. Nkpa, N. K. U. "Rumor mongering in war time." *Journal of Social Psychology* 96(1975): 27–35.
182. Odum, H. W. *Race and Rumors of Race*. Chapel Hill: University of North Carolina Press, 1943.
183. Oman, C. W. C. "Presidential address." *Transactions of the Royal Historical Society* Series IV (1918): 1–27.
184. O'Sullivan, R., and Brown, R. *The law of defamation*. London: Sweet & Maxwell, 1958.
185. Paine, R. "Gossip and transaction." *Man: The Journal of the Royal Anthropological Institute* 3, no. 2(1968): 305–8.
186. Paine, R. "Lappish decisions, partnerships, information management, and sanctions—a nomadic pastoral adaptation." *Ethnology* 9(1970): 52–67.
187. Payne, D. E., and Payne, K. P. "Newspapers and crime in Detroit." *Journalism Quarterly* 47(1970): 233–38.
188. Peterson, W. A., and Gist, N. P. "Rumor and public opinion." *American Journal of Sociology* 57(1951): 159–67.
189. Phelps, R. H., and Hamilton, E. D. *Libel, Rights, Risks, Responsibilities*. New York: Macmillan, 1966.
190. Polanyi, K.; Arensberg, C.; and Pearson, H. *Trade and Market in the Early Empires*. Glencoe, Illinois: Free Press, 1957.
191. Pollard, A. F. "Rumour and historical science in time of war." *Contemporary Revue* 107(1915): 321–30.
192. Ponsonby, A. *Falsehood in War-Time*. London: George Allen & Unwin, 1928.
193. Ponting, J. R. "Rumor control centers: their emergence and operations." *American Behavioral Scientist* 16(1973): 391–401.
194. Popkin, R. *The Second Oswald*. New York: Avon, 1966.
195. Powell, F. A. "Open- and closed-mindedness and the ability to differentiate source and message." *Journal of Abnormal and Social Psychology* 65(1962): 61–64.
196. Prasad, J. "The psychology of rumour: a study relating to the great Indian earthquake of 1934." *British Journal of Psychology* 26(1935): 1–15.
197. Prasad, J. "A comparative study of rumours and reports in earthquakes." *British Journal of Psychology* 41(1950): 129–44.

198. Radin, P. *Primitive Man as a Philosopher*. New York: Appleton, 1927.
199. Rapoport, A. "Spread of information through a population with socio-structural bias: I. assumptions of transitivity." *Bulletin of Mathematical Biophysics* 15(1953): 523–33.
200. Rapoport, A. "Spread of information through a population with socio-structural bias: II. various models with partial transitivity." *Bulletin of Mathematical Biophysics* 15(1953): 535–46.
201. Rapoport, A., and Rebhun, L. I. "On the mathematical theory of rumor spread." *Bulletin of Mathematical Biophysics* 14(1952): 375–83.
202. Redl, F. "The phenomenon of contagion and 'shock effect' in group therapy." *Searchlights on Delinquency*, edited by K. R. Eissler. New York: International Universities Press, 1949.
203. Reik, T. *Masochism in Modern Man*. New York: Farrar & Rinehart, 1941.
204. Riesman, D. *The Lonely Crowd*. New Haven: Yale University Press, 1950.
205. Riesman, D., and Roseborough, H. "Careers and consumer behavior." *Consumer Behavior*, edited by L. Clark. New York: New York University Press, 1955.
206. Roberts, J. M. "The self-management of cultures." *Explorations in Cultural Anthropology: Essays in Honor of George Peter Murdock*, edited by W. H. Goodenough. New York: McGraw-Hill, 1964.
207. Rolph, C. H. "Rumors." *The New Statesman and Nation*, February 19, 1944.
208. Roos, A. J. "The scuttle butt afloat: a study in group psychology." *Archives of Neurology and Psychiatry* 50(1943): 472–74.
209. Rose, A. M. "Rumor in the stock market." *Public Opinion Quarterly* 15(1951): 461–86.
210. Rosen, S., and Tesser, A. "On reluctance to communicate undesirable information: the MUM effect." *Sociometry* 33(1970): 253–63.
211. Rosenthal, M. "Where rumor raged." *Trans-Action* 8, no. 4(1971): 34–43.
212. Rosnow, R. L. "Poultry and prejudice." *Psychology Today* 5, no. 10(1972): 53–56.
213. Rosnow, R. L. "On rumor." *Journal of Communication* 24, no. 3(1974): 26–38.
214. Rosnow, R. L., and Fine, G. A. "Inside rumors." *Human Behavior* 3, no. 8(1974): 64–68.
215. Rosnow, R. L., and Robinson, E. J. *Experiments in Persuasion*. New York: Academic Press, 1967.
216. Rosten, L. *The Joys of Yiddish*. New York: McGraw-Hill, 1968.
217. Rubin, B. *Media Politics*. New York: Oxford, in preparation.
218. Ruch, F. L., and Young, K. "Penetration of axis propaganda." *Journal of Applied Psychology* 26(1942): 448–55.
219. Samovar, L. A. "A study of ambiguity and unequivocation in the

1960 presidential campaign debates." Doctoral dissertation, Purdue University, 1962. University Microfilms 62–3483.

220. Samovar, L. A. "Ambiguity and unequivocation in the Kennedy-Nixon television debates: a rhetorical analysis." *Western Speech* Fall(1965): 211–18.

221. Schachter, S., and Burdick, H. "A field experiment on rumor transmission and distortion." *Journal of Abnormal and Social Psychology* 50(1955): 363–71.

222. Schall, H. M.; Levy, B.; and Tresselt, M. E. "A sociometric approach to rumor." *Journal of Social Psychology* 31(1950): 121–29.

223. Schoenstein, R. "It was just a joke, folks." *TV Guide*, May 18, 1974, pp. 6–7.

224. Schuler, E. A., and Parenton, V. J. "A recent epidemic of hysteria in a Louisiana high school." *Journal of Social Psychology* 17(1943): 221–35.

225. Schultz, D. P. *Panic Behavior*. New York: Random House, 1964.

226. Sherif, M., and Sherif, C. W. *Social Psychology*. New York: Harper & Row, 1969.

227. Shibutani, T. *Improvised News: A Sociological Study of Rumor.* Indianapolis: Bobbs-Merrill, 1966.

228. Silverman, I. "On the resolution and tolerance of cognitive inconsistency in a natural-occurring event: attitudes and beliefs following the Senator Edward M. Kennedy incident." *Journal of Personality and Social Psychology* 17(1971): 171–78.

229. Sinha, D. "Behaviour in a catastrophic situation: a psychological study of reports and rumours." *British Journal of Psychology* 43(1952): 200–209.

230. Sinha, D. "Rumours as a factor in public opinion during elections." *The Eastern Anthropologist* 8(1955): 63–73.

231. Smelser, N. *Theory of Collective Behavior*. New York: Free Press, 1962.

232. Smith, G. F., and Dorfman, D. D. "The effect of stimulus uncertainty on the relationship between frequency of exposure and liking." *Journal of Personality and Social Psychology* 31(1975): 150–55.

233. Smith, G. H. "Beliefs in statements labeled fact and rumor." *Journal of Abnormal and Social Psychology* 42(1947): 80–90.

234. Smock, C. D. "The influence of psychological stress on the 'intolerance of ambiguity'." *Journal of Abnormal and Social Psychology* 50(1955): 177–82.

235. Sobel, R. *Amex: A History of the American Stock Exchange, 1921–1971*. New York: Weybright & Talley, 1972.

236. Stang, D. J. "Effects of 'mere exposure' on learning and affect." *Journal of Personality and Social Psychology* 31(1975): 7–12.

237. Stirling, R. B. "Some psychological mechanisms operative in gossip." *Social Forces* 34(1956): 262–67.

238. Suczek, B. "The curious case of the 'death' of Paul McCartney." *Urban Life and Culture* 1(1972): 61–76.

239. Sutton, H. "The grapevine: a study of role behavior within an

informal communication system." Doctoral dissertation, University of California, Berkeley, 1969.

240. Sutton, H., and Porter, L. W. "A study of the grapevine in a governmental organization." *Personnel Psychology* 21(1968): 223–30.

241. Szwed, J. F. "Gossip, drinking, and social control: consensus and communication in a Newfoundland parish." *Ethnology* 5(1966): 434–41.

242. Tannenbaum, P. H. "The congruity principle revisited: studies in the reduction, induction, and generalization of persuasion." *Advances in Experimental Social Psychology*, edited by L. Berkowitz, vol. 3, New York: Academic Press, 1967.

243. Tapp, J. L. "Children can understand rumor." *Social Education* 18(1953): 163–65.

244. Tapp, J. L. "Pictures help children conduct a 'rumor clinic'." *Educational Screen* 32, no. 1(1953): pp. 20 ff.

245. Taylor, J. A. "A personality scale of manifest anxiety." *Journal of Abnormal and Social Psychology* 48(1953): 285–90.

246. Thibaut, J. W., and Kelley, H. H. *The Social Psychology of Groups.* New York: Wiley, 1959.

247. Thomas, B. *Winchell.* New York: Berkeley Medalion Books, 1971.

248. Thomas, E. C. *The Law of Libel and Slander and Related Action.* Dobbs Ferry, New York: Oceana Publications, 1973.

249. Thomas, W. I., and Znaniecki, F. *The Polish Peasant in Europe and America.* New York: Knopf, 1927.

250. Thurston, E. T. "Both doing well." *McClure's Magazine,* June, 1915.

251. Tiffany, W. R., and Bennett, D. N. "Phonetic distortions in the serial transmission of short speech samples." *Journal of Speech and Hearing Research* 11(1968): 33–48.

252. Turner, R. H., and Killian, L. M. *Collective Behavior.* Englewood Cliffs: Prentice-Hall, 1957.

253. Turow, J. "Talk show radio as interpersonal communication." *Journal of Broadcasting* 18(1974): 171–79.

254. Ward, B. *Spaceship Earth.* New York: Columbia University Press, 1966.

255. Waters, H. F. "Public or private lives?" *Newsweek,* February 17, 1975, pp. 83–84.

256. Watson, J. D. *The Double Helix: Being a Personal Account of the Discovery of the Structure of DNA.* New York: Atheneum, 1968.

257. West, S. G.; Gunn, S. P.; and Chernicky, P. "Ubiquitous Watergate: an attributional analysis." *Journal of Personality and Social Psychology* 32(1975): 55–65.

258. Wheeler, L. "Toward a theory of behavioral contagion." *Psychological Review* 73(1966): 179–92.

259. Whipple, G. M. "The observer as reporter: a survey of the psychology of testimony." *Psychological Bulletin* 6(1909): 153–70.

260. White, D. M. "The 'gate keeper': a case study in the selection of news." *Journalism Quarterly* 27(1950): 383–90.
261. Williams, A. "TV's 'first war': unbiased study of television news bias." *Journal of Communication* 25(1975): 190–99.
262. Williams, L., and Erchak, G. "Rumor control centers in civil disorders." *Police Chief* (1969): 26–32.
263. Wittels, D. G. "Hitler's short-wave rumor factory." *Saturday Evening Post*, 1942, vol. 215, pp. 12–13, 118–123.
264. Worchel, S.; Lee, J.; and Adewole, A. "Effects of supply and demand on ratings of object value." *Journal of Personality and Social Psychology* 32(1975): 906–14.
265. Wulf, F. "Beiträge zur Psychologie der Gestalt: Über die Veränderung von Vorstellungen (Gedächtnis und Gestalt)." *Psychologische Forchung* 1(1922): 333–73.
266. Zaidi, S. M. H. "An experimental study of distortion in rumor." *Indian Journal of Social Work* 19(1958): 211–15.
267. Zajonc, R. F. "Attitudinal effects of mere exposure." *Journal of Personality and Social Psychology* 9, part 2(1968).
268. Zerner, E. H. "Rumors in Paris newspapers." *Public Opinion Quarterly* 10(1946): 382–91.

Index

Paine, R., 5, [77]
Parade magazine, 99
Parenton, V. J., [34]
Parsons, Louella, 89
Paul, Prince of Yugoslavia, 25
Payne, D. E., 105
Payne, K. P., 105
Pearson, Drew, 89
Pearson, H., [89]
Peltz, A. A., 134
Pennsylvania Gazette, 87
Pentagon Papers, 58
People magazine, 99
Peterson, W. A., [23]
Phelps, R. H., [125]
Philadelphia, murder in Society
    Hill, 55–6
Playboy magazine, 99
Polanyi, K., [89]
Political rumors and gossip,
    10–11, 27ff, 42, 83, 88, 97, 99,
    115ff (*see also* Kennedy; Nixon;
    Watergate)
Pollard, A. F., [43]
Ponsonby, A., [24]
Ponting, J. R., [45], [122]
Popkin, R., [19]
Porter, L. W., [35]
Postman, L. J., [12], 16, 28, 30, 37,
    39–40, 51–2, 63, 68–9, [97], 101,
    103, 132
Powell, F. A., [46]
Prasad, J., [23], [29]
Profumo affair, 100 (*see also*
    Keeler)
Project Revere, 32ff
Pyle, Howard, 82

Quarles, Francis, 107
Queen Mary, H.M.S., 120

Radin, P., [55]
Random House Dictionary, 12, 83
Rapoport, A., 35

Reader's Digest, 23
Rebhun, L. I., [35]
Redl, F., [35]
Reik, T., 92
Remembering, 37–8
*Report of the National Advisory
    Commission on Civil Disorders*,
    12, 134–5 (*see also* Kerner)
Restle, F., [54]
"Revolution Number 9", 14
Riesman, D., [88]
Roberts, J. M., [93]
Robinson, E. J., [24], [117]
Robinson, W. H., 110–1
Rolph, C. H., [27]
Roos, A. J., 56
Roosevelt Franklin D., 89
Rose, A. M., [29], [79]
Roseborough, H., [88]
Rosen, S., [41]
Rosenthal, M., [4], [47–8]
Rosnow, R. L., [13], [24], [44],
    [47–8], 69ff, [74], [75], [105],
    [117]
Rosten, Leo, [12], 81
Rubin, B., 105, 126
Ruch, F. L., [24]
Rumor
    belief in, factors affecting,
        75ff
    classification, 23–4, 57, 131
    definition, 11, 130
    etymology, 9
    life cycle stages
        adventures, 31ff
        birth, 22
        death, 42ff
    theoretical explanations
        eclectic, 57ff
        neural synapse model,
            32, 72, 132
        psychological, 51ff
        sociological, 54ff